STOP SMOKING IN

ONE HOUR

Valerie Austin

JOHN BLAKE

Published by John Blake Publishing Ltd,
3 Bramber Court, 2 Bramber Road,
London W14 9PB, England

First published in 2000

ISBN 1 85782 441 5

British Library Cataloguing-in-Publication Data:

A catalogue record for this book is
available from the British Library.

Typeset by t2

Printed in Great Britain by
Creative Print and Design (Wales),
Ebbw Vale, Gwent.

1 3 5 7 9 10 8 6 4 2

Papers used by John Blake Publishing are natural, recyclable
products made from wood grown in sustainable forests. The
manufacturing processes conform to the environmental
regulations of the country of origin.

CONTENTS

ACKNOWLEDGEMENTS

For the person who found the research that was supressed for so long – my partner, historian and author James Pool.

Gil Boyne for his help through the years and for introducing me to this magnificent world of the mind.

Peter Coady, long-term friend for his unconditional loyalty and support.

Tom and crew for their artful public relations.

I am most grateful for help received in many forms from Kevin James and Brenda El-Leithy, who interrrupted their already busy schedules to help with last-minute changes.

Members of my Association of Advanced Hynotherapists for their support with my researches.

Roy Stockdill, my friend, agent and support.

Aaron Eldan, for sharing his research and supplying me with US and Canadian information.

John Blake for having the foresight to publish this material.

The Malaysian connection ...

The wonderful help and kindness I have

received:

Datuk Lee Kim Sai, former Minister of Health for his acceptance and support.

Prof. Dato.

Dr Abdul Halim Othman, Dean, Faculty of Science Social and Humanities, National University of Malaysia for his recognition, trust, and for giving me the honour of training his students of psychology at the University.

The *New Straits Times* for their support over the years and their well-written articles.

The people of the beautiful paradise island of Langkawi where my book was started. The staff at the splendid hotels that hosted my Learning In Paradise courses.

My long-term friend Siti Baizura Husin whose invaluable hospitality and help played an important part in my visits.

And of course all my students and clients around the world.

PREFACE

Although few people, even professors and academics it seems, are aware of the fact, there are thousands of scholarly studies on hypnosis. Extensive research has been carried out on hypnosis for smoking cessation.

The most successful study on the use of hypnosis to stop smoking was carried out by Von Dedenroth in his report entitled 'The Use of Hypnosis in 1000 Tobacco Maniacs', he maintained a 94% success rate for 18 months or more. Kline reported an 88% success rate based on a one-year follow-up. Watkins, Sanders, and Crasilneck and Hall all reported success rates in their studies of 67–68% with follow-ups ranging from six months to one year.* I have listed 20 important research papers and academic books in the bibliography.

Have these results simply been ignored? Certain national pharmaceutical corporations believe that their products, such as Nicotine replacement patches, gum tablets and sprays, have a better success rate than other alternatives. However, hypnosis has a much higher success rate in stopping smoking than patches, gum and all the

* For a summary of the success rates of various studies of hypnosis and smoking see Brown & Fromm *Hypnosis and Behavioural Medecine*, p167

rest. Hypnosis is not a drug and there is no evidence of any negative side effects from it.

Suppression of information on cigarette smoking and its dangers are not new. As the film *The Insider* starring Al Pacino showed, tobacco drug companies have what seemed unlimited money and willingly used part of it in an attempt to break a powerful television network. The bravery and determination of two men broke the story and the programme *Sixty Minutes* was left with a badly tainted reputation for their part in suppressing information about the harm cigarrettes can cause.

What is hypnosis? The word 'hypnotherapy' means therapy while you are in hypnosis. Hypnosis is a deep state of relaxation. The techniques used in the therapy and not the hypnosis itself determine the success rate. So if someone says, 'I have had hypnotherapy and it did not work', this would be as impractical as saying, 'I went to school and it didn't work because I didn't pass my exams.' A student, however, would be influenced by the teacher and the method used by the teacher to teach.

Hypnosis has been scientifically proven to be the most successful method of smoking cessation, even with just 'suggestion' hypnosis. So why is this fact not publicly reported? It is very easy for scientific studies and their data to get lost in the global consciousness when the media does not take an interest. The information goes unreported, buried in files and is known only to the choice few that happen to read it in scholarly journals or more accessible magazines such as the *New Scientist*.

This book is written for the person who intends to give up smoking. It is also useful for the person who is unsure about quitting and may just need that extra nudge to enable them to decide to quit and save their and/or your health. I am not writing with the intention of being judgmental, but to give you, the reader, the facts and benefit of my experience of treating more than 3,000 smokers around the world. My observations may dispel some of the theories that have been accepted as facts. You can stop smoking in one hour, or as long as it takes to play the tape that you prepared from the instructions provided. But, read this book first; it will greatly increase your chances of success.

In this book you will find an explanation of how the mind functions and why you are facing difficulties in giving up smoking. It will give you some facts on new and exciting hypnotherapy, proven in research but only now filtering through to the public through some well-informed documentaries. I have written this information from my personal experiences rather than just by using facts and figures at random. I hope it proves useful to you. The knowledge will help expand your mind from 'I cannot' to 'I can'.

Knowledge creates growth and the following pages are filled with information that I believe you will find empowering. I have been fortunate to be in a position where specific knowledge has been offered to me by the many great people who have passed through my life. I can say without any doubt that my techniques work, and am able to reflect on years of success as one of Britain's leaders in stop-smoking therapy. Smoking is not a bad habit. It may be unhealthy, but it is not bad, until you decide to give it up and find you can't – then it becomes a bad habit. You do not practise something you do not want to do, and in order to become a smoker it takes a certain amount of practice. When you decide to become a smoker, you do so because you choose to. You may have wanted to do it in the beginning because it was grown up, or sociable. You may have believed that it would give you confidence or, in very unusual cases (and this happened to my son at boarding school), it may be forced upon you. In my son's case, it was part of the initiation ceremony at school. Both habit and trauma in smoking problems will be covered in this book.

To help the smoker give up smoking I have a website that has a free audio of my hypnosis suggestion, and you may find it useful to listen to this when you are taping your own suggestion as instructed in chapter one.

1

INTRODUCTION TO HYPNOSIS

'Because smoking is a psychological addiction, tablets or nicotine replacement products cannot address the mental addiction. Creating a change of attitude by hypnosis effectively changes the physiological behaviour of your body.'

You may be interested in stopping smoking, or you may be the person who wants someone close to you to stop. In order to be less confusing and yet still cater to both readers, I have written this book addressing the smoker, and hopefully the passive smoker will bear with me. Rather than be judgmental, and because I only treat smokers who want to stop, I will attempt to show you how the mind works and why you are experiencing such resistance in giving up a habit you no longer want. I have included facts from around the world that are intended to give you a stronger commitment to quitting smoking, and facts on why you haven't been able to – yet! Or you may just need that little extra push to help you to decide to quit smoking, and save your health and even your life (or at least, to help you have a better quality of life). The benefits are vast, but one very important incentive is freedom. Freedom from a habit you no longer want. My observations may surprise you but the intention is to dispel some of the theories that seem to have been adopted as fact.

My goal is to offer you the opportunity to Stop Smoking in One Hour, or even sooner. The book is designed to give you a simplified and practical explanation on how and why the mind is resistant to you stopping; to help you build up your belief system and enable you to be more open to positive suggestions and instructions to allow a change in your attitude. If you change your attitude, your behaviour will automatically change.

Please try to avoid shortcuts by skipping these very important chapters, as so many

people do in their excitement to speed up the process. These words are designed to give you the facts to encourage your conscious mind to work with you. The result is less 'noise' when you are trying to relax. The 'noise' is the conversation that your mind has with itself when you are making changes. So the extra time invested here at the beginning will give you a far better success rate.

In the following chapters you will find detailed explanations and examples to help you understand why you are in such a dilemma. You will find facts on this new and exciting therapy, proven in research but only now filtering through to the public through some well-informed documentaries. I have gathered much of the information from my personal experiences and academic statistics from acceptable and reliable sources. This knowledge is intended to help expand your mind to allow you to change from 'I can't' to 'I can'.

Let's first look at the habit rather than the addiction!

More proof that my techniques work is that my one-to-one therapy can be taught to the business person who would like a profession in stopping people smoking, and they too can have the same high success rate. However, the self-help therapy taught in this book in itself has a higher success rate than anything else on the market, apart from the one-to-one therapy(as explained in the preface).

For whatever the reason, and the list of possible causes is incredibly long, you make the decision to practise so that you can become a smoker. Even if your memory is conveniently edited, you will still have had to practise simply because the body is not designed to accept the assault of smoke without objection, e.g. coughing, dizziness, feeling slightly sick, or simply reacting to the unpleasant taste of a cigarette. Even the person who persists in believing that they enjoyed their first cigarette will reveal a very different story when they are taken back, in hypnosis, to experience again their true sensations at the event. It is usually quite a surprise when you experience the actual distaste and the awkwardness of trying to force an alien substance in your lungs.

Smoking only becomes a *bad* habit when you decide to stop and find you can't. Why does a smoker who wants to stop believe he or she can't? What is preventing them? Why do they smoke? 'I enjoy it', was the reply from many a smoker that came to see me in Harley Street for treatment that would help them to stop. This remark was contradictory, particularly after they had given me a string of major disadvantages that belied this belief.

If a person gives a logical answer to a question, but the answer doesn't match their actions, then that person is working on an incorrect programme. To test it, ask yourself if you are doing something that you don't want to do, but are doing it anyway. If this is the case, then the quickest way to re-programme yourself is with hypnosis, thus avoiding a long and arduous battle resulting from an inner conflict. This rule is not just confined to smoking, but in the smoker it is more noticeable. Hypnosis allows you to eliminate an unwanted habit without the need to practise out of it, as would normally be the case.

So why does the smoker believe they smoke because they enjoy it, having made the decision to stop and having taken time to carefully work out all the reasons that they dislike the habit? It is simply because the conscious mind does not have an answer to the question 'Why do I smoke?' It does not know why the person is smoking when he or she no longer wants to, so therefore it fabricates an answer that will satisfy that person – an answer that is logical and sounds acceptable. The conscious mind doesn't know the answer, because it is not involved with the way in which a habit is formed. It simply recognises the procedure – that there is now a new habit.

When I first started training people in advanced hypnotherapy, a stage hypnotist explained a particular trick that he used to me, and it gave me an insight into how the mind is so easily fooled. He would invite a volunteer on stage, and then he would give a suggestion while the volunteer was in hypnosis. The suggestion was for the person to return to their seat, take off their shoes and change them round so they would be on the wrong feet. The volunteer would then be told to forget these instructions. On returning to their seat they would follow the instructions and change their shoes. They were oblivious to the sniggering of the crowd because they simply didn't associate it with themselves. When the hypnotist asked them why they had changed shoes, the subconscious would immediately give a reasonable reason: 'My shoes are too tight' was a favourite answer. If they were told that they had been instructed to do this in hypnosis, they would not believe it. To convince them you would have to show them a video of themselves in hypnosis, with the suggestion being given. So, is this why the smoker says he or she likes to smoke when asked why they are smoking? Is it that the conscious mind has merely found an acceptable explanation that seems reasonable consciously and is rarely questioned?

We have all seen, or heard, about the hypnotist who gives a volunteer a lemon or an onion, and suggests to them, while they are in hypnosis, that it is a juicy orange that they can't wait to eat. The subconscious sends the signal out that it is a juicy orange and the volunteer is convinced enough to take big bites out of the onion or lemon. Until, that is, they are brought out of hypnosis and realise what it is they are really eating. The likely response will be to promptly spit out the offending piece of onion or lemon.

With hypnosis, it is a simple task to change a desirable taste to an unpleasant one, or a sophisticated pose to one that is ridiculous, or vice versa. I once saw a hypnotist give an instruction to a lady that she would only get satisfaction by smoking from her elbow. She managed this ridiculous stance quite easily, receiving the same satisfaction from the cigarette even though it was not even in her mouth! She breathed in with an expression of bliss on her face, oblivious to the fact that she wasn't even getting any nicotine, only psychological satisfaction, which was undoubtedly enjoyable.

Since smoking is classed as a mental addiction, this is not surprising. You can experience the same side effects when you are trying to lose weight, stop drinking alcohol or even stop gambling. The gambler is not reliant on substances to give him an addiction – it's a purely psychological phenomenon. Simple hypnosis experiments prove that it's all in your attitude and how you perceive the situation at the time.

So how is a habit formed?

A habit is formed by practice. You do not practise something you do not choose to do. The subconscious is a function. I like to describe it as a very sophisticated robot. If you were to ask a man-made robot to make a cup of tea, it could do so easily with the equipment for which it had been programmed. However, if you bought an upgraded tea-maker for which the robot had not been programmed, it would not be able to perform the simple task of making tea.

To form a habit naturally it has to be demonstrated, and then practised, before the subconscious takes it on board. The practice demonstrates to the subconscious that you are serious, but with hypnosis the habit just needs to be demonstrated and programmed. The success rate is in the sophistication of programming. That is why some hypnotherapists have a much lower success rate than others. The range can be as low as 30% or as high as 95%.

If you decide to ride a bike, you have to practise. You consciously instruct your subconscious by simply going through the motions and repeating the process until you can. When you are eventually able to ride the bike you no longer do it consciously. It becomes a subconscious action, which means that, by definition, the conscious mind is no longer in control. You can request, or even try to demand, as hard as you like, that your mind stops the habit of smoking, nail biting, etc.

However, the conscious will carry on the programme, because this is what it is programmed to do, following a primal basic survival instinct.

The subconscious does not have to be judgmental and therefore it does not matter whether this habit is good for you or not. The subconscious reasoning is that if you practise something enough it must be what you want to do. After a certain amount of practice (very little in smoking), the subconscious takes the habit on board, eliminating the conscious involvement. This is fine and works extremely well, unless of course you decide you don't want this particular habit any more; then there is conflict in the mind. You are now doing something you 'don't' want to do and your conscious has no idea why you cannot change.

If you could get rid of a habit easily, then it could be a threat to your survival. Imagine if you were driving a car in busy traffic or on a motorway and you suddenly forgot how to drive. This could result in a serious or even fatal accident. If you were flying a commercial plane, coming into land, and you forgot the habit you had acquired of reading the instruments, you would find it very difficult to touch down safely. Imagine how inconvenient it would be if you learnt a second language and because you hadn't used it for some time, you completely forgot it and had to re-learn from scratch. It is necessary to keep habits to be used when you require them – they never disappear completely, they just stay dormant until you are ready to use them again. Since you don't normally practise something you don't want to learn, this works very well. Nail biting, thumb sucking, picking your nose, all these unpleasant habits may have been comforting at one time but later they became socially unacceptable, so you have to work at practising out of the habit. If you decide you want to resurrect a habit again, for example speaking a second language or riding a bike, maybe after ten years, you would respond to the old habit almost immediately. You may be a little shaky at first, but just by doing it, in a very short time you will become as good as ever.

Just so the smoker. If he or she has another cigarette, even years later, they will then become a smoker again. So remember, when you stop smoking, if you are ever tempted to have a cigarette just ask yourself, 'Do I want to be a smoker again?', because that's what will happen. You just awaken the habit once more – but it will be your choice.

As a smoker you will always have the habit of smoking. If you choose to start again after you have given up, you will get right back into your original habit within a couple of weeks. The good news is that you can stop, and stop permanently. Just because you have formed a habit doesn't mean to say that you have to practise it, just as you don't have to keep speaking another language when it is inappropriate. It's just there for your convenience and, as the old saying goes, "What you don't use you lose."

So how can you train your mind to form the habit of not smoking? The long and uncomfortable way is to practise out of it, The easy way is to use hypnosis, which means you do not need any practice at all. Why? Because you are accessing the subconscious directly and re-programming it. The subconscious part of the mind's function is to protect, not to destroy. This means that any suggestion you put in the script for your subconscious will not be accepted if it is derogatory or unworkable, e.g. that a broken leg will be fixed tomorrow. But it is still prudent to be precise, to prevent confusion, and that is why I have included a section on how to create a suggestion (see chapter 3).

It seems very unsophisticated in this modern era that the average person is surprised when told they are able to correct faulty behaviour patterns by using natural methods of mind control. It has been proved over and over again that hypnosis works and that, even in its most basic form, it has a higher success rate than any other method. It is only the percentage, in terms of the success rate, that fluctuates with the many varieties of techniques used in hypnosis.

If you overhear someone saying that they have had hypnosis and it didn't work, such a remark would be as silly as saying that they went to school, and it didn't work because they didn't pass their exams. How they faired at school would depend on the teacher and what method of teaching they used.

Is smoking an addiction or a habit?

The following information gives you the opportunity to question the many beliefs that have been bandied around for years, ones that you have accepted or thought to be true even though they may be totally unfounded. Because the research on smoking habits versus addictions is so mixed, one scientifically disproving a theory that has just been scientifically proved, we cannot say for certain whether smoking is an addiction or a habit or a bit of both. But we can say that if it is indeed an addiction, by using hypnosis the subconscious can nevertheless deal with it. After successful hypnosis, rarely does the ex-smoker have to go through the withdrawal symptoms that are usual to smokers trying to give up. At the very worst, any withdrawals are so slight that they are manageable or go unnoticed.

We can establish smoking as a *mental* addiction, so no wonder nicotine replacements have such a moderate success rate. It seems you need to chew 36 packs of gum to replace each pack of cigarettes you smoke in order to get a similar amount of nicotine. Even if you were to stick patches all over your body day and night it would still have little impact, apart from a small percentage above the placebo effect, certainly never reaching a puff of one cigarette. The nasal spray comes close to the hit of a cigarette, but has its drawbacks – it is probably more objectionable to use, and certainly less of a *pose*. It is designed more to help the passive smoker.

I would comfortably say that smoking could be both a physical and psychological addiction. I also believe that the physical addiction is very tame and can be easily overridden by hypnosis. This does not happen with such drugs as cocaine or heroin. You would need many more sessions with regression therapy (going back to the trauma event via hypnosis) to make changes. In one-to-one therapy using advanced hypnotherapy techniques you can achieve a percentage success rate in the high 90s in just one session. (Von Dedenroth, 1960, proved a 94% success rate after 18 months.) I have maintained a 95% success rate, as have many of the therapists I have trained. If you look at chapter 5 it will give you some surprising figures for success rates of products on the market that are designed to help you stop.

Now let us look at some of the excuses that the client gives for smoking. Remember that the subconscious has to generate a logical reason for you to smoke. A few years ago, some publicity about me in a national newspaper went under the headline 'I CAN STOP YOU SMOKING IN ONE HOUR'. Following such a positive headline, people from all over England, and even Scotland, were travelling to me for a consultation in Harley Street. They would travel all night to get to me for an early appointment. I became fully booked for one year just on the strength of this one article.

I would see people who were dying; one lady was told by her doctor that she would have to have her leg amputated if she carried on smoking. Even with this threat hanging over her she had not been able to stop. Add to this the fact that most surgeons were smoking – even after being constantly subjected to seeing the terribly damaged lungs of their patients.

The subconscious habit is very powerful, so do not believe that you are unusual in finding it difficult to stop the smoking habit. One of the US hypnotherapy companies that specialised in stopping smoking did a survey of its clients. They had noticed that some people found it more difficult to stop smoking than others. So they devised a questionnaire on which one of the main questions was to enquire if the smokers believed they had a smoking *habit* or if they believed it was an *addiction*.

Those who believed that they had an addiction had side effects when trying to stop. The others, who just believed that it was a habit, stopped easily and with no side effects. When tested scientifically, the ones that believed they had an addiction had activated one by belief alone. They had created a physical addiction while the others had not. The trauma-related smoker had even more unpleasant side effects when attempting to stop.

One of the techniques used for stopping smoking used in hypnosis is aversion therapy, where it is suggested to you, while you are in hypnosis, that the cigarette tastes of rubber or something equally offensive. When you return to a normal state, the cigarette repulses you as it reminds you of the rubber. This helps you to stop and by the time the suggestion has worn off it has given you that all-important period of time to realise that you do not need a cigarette. I have included a less offensive but equally effective aversion therapy in chapter 3.

When I visited a conference for Smoking Cessation in 1992, it included GPs and the National Health sector, as well as some private specialists.

The conference was to discuss smoking cessation treatment, with the intention of cutting down the national smokers by a healthy percentage. A variety of booths had been constructed in the conference hall, allowing each product to advertise their wares. Patches, then new on the market, gum, and sprays were prominent. It was interesting that hypnosis was not represented; it wasn't even on the agenda. Nor was it listed on the charts giving the percentages of success rate of the various treatments. In fact, it was as if hypnotherapy didn't exist. It is no wonder that doctors, not to mention the press, do not have the correct information about it, and so have little enthusiasm to recommend the most successful method on the market to date for helping smokers to kick the habit.

It is easy to bring forward research on drug-based alternatives, as the drug companies have the money to do so. When a conference is being set up, the organisers ask the companies to supply proof of their success, and this is where the drug companies are streets ahead. Most hypnotherapists do not have access to the reports and research on hypnotherapy that come out through the years, and of course if you ask a hypnotherapist who does not have the information it is presumed there is none. Therefore, the word goes forward that hypnosis has not been proven to stop people smoking. Yet if you ask any doctor he will generally say that hypnosis *can* be successful for some people, which doesn't give too much confidence, as he too will have little, if any, evidence in his medical training.

What else can I say except that it certainly does work and there is now proof, and that it is this easy transformation the smoker experiences when giving up smoking that keeps a hypnotherapist in business? The ex-smoker brings in a string of client referrals for all sorts of other ailments or irritations, i.e. weight, insomnia and even self-development by increasing productivity, because seeing a devout smoker stop, without a problem, and stay stopped, gives them the confidence in the therapy to try it out for themselves.

So how does the smoker get to quit?

The combination of four powerful techniques used in hypnosis, plus the important information in the following pages, has been designed specifically to give you the ultimate self-help package for stopping smoking. But just as important is your decision to stop this costly habit – this is your commitment.

When you allow yourself to go into hypnosis, after reading this book, you will have more information about the dangers of smoking and why the mind tends to sabotage the process of stopping a habit – a habit that could actually kill you. This means you will have the tools to succeed, to achieve your goal of being a non-smoker, as if you had never smoked. When you have stopped smoking by hypnosis you will find that you look back on your smoking days not as a problem, but as a period you have grown out of. Your attitude will have changed. Think of the days at school or college when you had to behave in a certain way that made you feel important. Looking back, you can see that that was simply how you felt at the time. Now you are an adult and have a different attitude. You could compare it with putting new updated software in your 'mind' computer to enable you to operate a more sophisticated programme. The suggestions you choose to use in hypnosis (covered in chapter 3) will then give you a basis to help your subconscious to accept the new programme. The subconscious is compelled to help you to survive; smoking is a threat to your life, and hinders simple basic functions such as breathing with ease.

In chapter 3 you will find a variety of suggestions to suit many types of smokers, and there are some basic rules of the mind that are given to help you form your own designer script. Whatever treatment or method you use to stop smoking, it will never take away your choice permanently. However, the good news is that hypnosis is intended to change your attitude so that you no longer need to use the habit of smoking. You simply do not wish to.

It's not how many or how long

When a person comes to me to be treated in order to stop smoking I ask three questions:

1. How many cigarettes do you smoke?
2. When did you start?
3. Why do you want to stop now?

When I have established the number of cigarettes

they smoke a day, I then explain that the quantity of cigarettes smoked a day makes no difference to them stopping smoking. Neither does the number of years they have smoked have any significance in them giving up. Whether they have smoked for only a few months or for 70 years, this has no bearing on the matter. They are either a smoker or not. I then establish the reasons, which can be many and varied, for giving up at that time. The age just gives me an indication of when they started. However, the most important question that affects the therapy is why they want to stop. You need to want to do it for yourself and not because your partner/parents want you to. It is your decision and if you want to stop that is good enough.

I had a client who was an author and who came to my office with a smoking habit of five cigarettes a day. I looked at her and said, quite unprepared for the answer, 'That's not much!' Her reply took me aback: 'It is to me!' I had been seeing smokers for two years and she was the first who was smoking so little as a habit, and yet acted like a heavy smoker. She had decided to cut down and it wasn't working at all. In fact, this lady was responsible for me putting together a very successful excessive social drinking treatment as I shall explain in chapter 6.

Her smoking was linked to her work and she believed she wouldn't be able to concentrate or even create her stories as well without smoking. On the surface she believed she smoked to relieve the stress of deadlines. It can be a very solitary profession to be a successful writer, especially when you are working on novels. The author was very pleased to be released from her unwanted habit and later went on to learn my speed-reading technique with hypnosis. It emphasised the fact that if you can stop a bad habit without needing to practise out of it then you can create a new positive habit, also without the need to practise. On my training courses I train speed-reading on the second day so that the student therapists can read through the manual in the evenings during the course. I can guarantee doubling a person's reading speed with at least the same retention. This has been invaluable on my courses.

Stress does not prevent you from stopping smoking

My first introduction to the stock exchange gave

me the proof I needed that you can stop smoking just as easily, whether you have a stressful job or not. My first client from the stock exchange was young, successful and very bright. He had little belief that hypnotherapy would work and only came to me as a last hope. He, of course, stopped and, just as I had expected, approximately a month later, when his business colleagues had had time to satisfy themselves he wasn't going to start again, the referrals began. Within the next six months I had seen over 60 people from the same company. I had to have an excellent reputation for so many to book in for therapy. If one or two started smoking again it would have affected future referrals. This gave some indication that a stressful profession has little to do with the intention to stop smoking. There is never a good time to stop, so there is nothing to prevent you stopping now.

Sleep Hypnosis

Bernheim, an eminent doctor in the 1880s, induced hypnosis with many of his patients in hospital while they were asleep and it proved very successful. It is possible that even this was predated by a hundred years, as it was suggested the mesmerists may have used it.

I have introduced sleep hypnosis in this book to explain its availability as a self-hypnosis alternative to advanced therapy, and if the stop-smoking suggestions in the book seem to be insufficient due to hidden trauma. Fortunately, a trauma-based smoking habit is extremely rare – this therapy is an added tool to give you the maximum success rate. A little more on trauma based smoking is covered in chapter 6.

Sleep hypnosis is a technique to contact the inner mind when you are asleep. It is a different technique and seems to operate on a deeper section of the mind, as if it is contacting the inner self rather than just the subconscious. This means that the words used in normal suggestion hypnosis would be not as effective because the approach is completely different.

The instruction at the beginning allows the mind to listen and operate while the person is sleeping; without such words the success rate drops considerably. It is different from our usual understanding of subliminal, in fact a totally new approach, as you have been brought into a different type of sleep. I found that it worked for me after the death of my father five years ago. I was suffering the dreadful loss and had a raw guilt that had been established from nightmare incidents and shocks during the past 25 years. I had my share of intensive therapy and was reluctant to go digging again. I flew to the US especially to attend a workshop at Gil Boyne's annual hypnotherapy convention, where I had some personal therapy. It quite amazes me that when someone wants to have specialist help for important problems, smoking or other restrictive behaviour, some of which may even save their life – they still expect there to be a specialist in their local area. If you wanted to have a facelift I'm sure you wouldn't pick someone down the road. You would probably go to London, or find wherever the best surgeon was practising.

These conventions and workshops around the world help the practitioner to keep up to date with their skills. The knowledge I gain means I can pass it directly on to my students. That is why I am so confident in recommending the therapists I train.

I met Jack Mason, an old friend and one of the established hypnotherapists, at such a conference in California. Jack also introduced me to third party healing, even deeper than sleep hypnosis – a method where a volunteer, who is used to going into hypnotic trance, is taken extremely deep, far deeper than generally used for trance. To test the level of trance, you count the volunteer's breaths per minute and, when they get to a certain number, you know they are at the correct depth to send energy/healing to the third party – rather like a mind e-mail with an attachment. The 'sender' is conserving energy by going into a type of hibernation state, releasing the build-up of 'fuel/memory' or whatever you would like to call it to send concentrated extra energy to help the 'recipient' heal.

The fascinating part is that the person you are sending the energy to can be in a coma, and results can be tracked on the monitoring equipment in the hospital. I was able to use this type of therapy in an intensive care unit in London when a patient was dying. Her husband reported, 'I was watching my wife lying on the table, dying. She was given 40 litres of blood. They kept transfusing blood into her and it just came straight out. They managed to stop the bleeding but because she had completely new blood, it had no fight in it. She caught an infection and her temperature began to soar. The doctors prepared me for the loss of my wife.'

I was called to the hospital and used a combination of hypnosleep and very deep hypnosis on the dying woman. This process allowed me literally to send her the extra energy I had conserved by being in this hibernating type of trance. It worked and only took minutes. Her temperature, which was unhealthily high, started to drop comfortably. The event was reported in the newspapers and an article, entitled 'Hypnotherapy saves woman's life in hospital drama', featured in the *Lancaster Guardian*, Friday April 14, 2000.

So if you can help save someone's life through the power of hypnosis, you can surely help someone to stop smoking.

2

IN A TRANCE

I will begin by explaining in detail the different stages of trance. This will enable you to gain a better understanding of what is happening to you or your subject when they are experiencing hypnosis. For the purpose of this explanation, I will call the person being hypnotised the 'subject'. If you have no one to assist you, then you will be hypnotising yourself by a tape recording, and you will be the 'subject'.

For suggestion hypnosis, any of these stages are adequate. It is only when you require the subject to participate in therapy, by either lifting an arm or talking to you while in hypnosis, that it would be useful to study more. It was only ignorance that caused a fear of hypnosis in the first place and it is only ignorance that still fuels any fear today.

All trance states are hypnosis, but there are different stages or depths of trance encouraging a different response. I have purposely omitted the various scientific theories and just presented you with some easy to understand facts.

You are either in hypnosis or not. It's a little bit like pregnancy – you are either pregnant or not. However, with practice you can go into deeper states that allow you to attain internal healing. Some people go immediately into deep hypnosis and others take a little longer to attain the state, but everyone can be hypnotised if they want to be. Just like everyone can learn to ride a bike – but some people take a little longer to learn and they have to practise more.

1. The Light Trance

The light trance is when the mind and body are relaxed enough to slow the mind down so that it can clearly focus on imagination. In this form of trance you can work easily with both suggestion and more advanced therapy. You can even achieve partial amnesia and it is also excellent for accelerated learning. Your conscious isn't battling with the new material, logically analysing the new information. The conscious mind just sits back and allows this fresh data to flow through into the subconscious mind reasonably unrestricted, just like it does with a four-year-old child.

There are certain physical changes that occur when a person is in hypnosis. For example, eyelids rapidly fluttering, relaxed muscle tone, changes in skin colour, as if in sleep. If you instruct the client to open their eyes while in hypnosis, the whites of their eyes can look very pink for a second or two, due to the eye muscles totally relaxing. There are many indications that a person is in trance, but they can be very misleading, and the subject may not show any noticeable symptoms whilst still in deep hypnosis. Therefore I have just briefly mentioned them here so that you are aware of their existence.

2. Somnambulism

The Marquis de Puysegur, a student of Mesmer, discovered the phenomenon of somnambulism, a deeper trance, in the 1800s. The mind is completely relaxed either by a group of instructions in the form of a suggestion, or occasionally by some subjects going directly into this state spontaneously. To achieve this state by suggestion, the semantics used are very important and need to be consistent. The word somnambulism in hypnosis terms shouldn't be confused with the dictionary explanation of sleepwalking.

Also called 'waking' hypnosis, the stage hypnotist relies on this depth of trance, as the subject can talk, open their eyes and still carry out everyday tasks. A popular demonstration to prove the phenomenon of trance is to ask a hypnotised subject to pick a number between 1 and 10. The hypnotist then instructs the subject to eliminate the number from their memory, and forget the instruction has been given. The subconscious will carry out the suggestion, as it presents no threat to the person involved. It would not act on an instruction that would be too embarrassing or harmful to the subject's individual standards.

The suggestion given when a subject is in somnambulism shows how the mind can follow outside influences, such as in this case, causing partial amnesia. When the subject is asked to open their eyes, they are then instructed to count their fingers. Invariably, they miss the number they have been asked to forget and end up with one finger spare. They look totally bemused, not knowing how they have managed to miscalculate.

3. The 'Coma' Trance (Dave Elman)

The coma state is a much deeper state of hypnosis. It is the only state in which the subject is catatonic. This means that you can move the subject's arms into any position, however uncomfortable it may look, and it will stay there until you move it again. The limb feels waxy, more pliable. The subject experiences lethargy and is completely and wonderfully relaxed and their whole body is fully anaesthetised.

The coma state, unless used for painless surgery, is of little use for advanced forms of hypnotherapy because the subject will not respond to physical suggestions or be able to answer questions. To the stage hypnotist it is a menace. Because it is such a marvellous state for the subject, they simply do not want to be disturbed. Before a method for terminating this trance was discovered, the hypnotist would try to remove the subject from the stage as quickly as possible. They would usually fail to bring the person out of trance, which would upset and worry the audience.

Although very uncommon, and most unlikely, a subject can go directly into the coma state immediately they are hypnotised. This state was where the fear of hypnosis originated – that a subject could be 'stuck' in hypnosis. If left alone, the subject will naturally come out of trance, just as if they were daydreaming, and it is no more harmful. The most successful suggestion to terminate this type of trance is to say, 'If you don't come out of hypnosis you will never be able to go into hypnosis again.' Because it is so gentle a threat it always brings the subject out of hypnosis.

So How Do You Hypnotise Yourself?

There are three types of induction that can be used to sufficiently relax a person into hypnosis: shock, confusion and boredom. The instant induction, which has a shock element and is immediate, looks very impressive for demonstrations, taking only seconds to induce full relaxation. The rapid induction, which basically confuses the mind and overloads it, presents a more gentle approach, but still takes less than a minute to induce. The progressive induction really bores the mind into hypnosis. It is considered to be the most reliable form of induction and is usually used for self-hypnosis. This traditional method can take quite some time and the longest one outlined in this book takes approximately twelve minutes.

THE TECHNIQUE FOR SELF-HYPNOSIS

1. An understanding of the method you use (in these chapters)

2. Progressive Relaxation – a comfortable set of words to induce the trance state.

3. A suggestion that is an 'instruction' while in a trance state.

4. Count out of hypnosis. To leisurely ease you out of trance. However, without it you will automatically come out of trance, the same as you would a daydream.

5. Practice.

6. Tests for visualisation (p84).

The following instructions are for the volunteer who is guiding the self-hypnosis. If you don't have a volunteer, you can follow the instructions and record your own voice on a tape recorder and play it back when you are sitting or lying down comfortably. I have purposely excluded any instructions for the instant and rapid inductions as they are more advanced techniques, but I have introduced them here so that you are aware they exist.

THE THREE TYPES OF INDUCTIONS

The instant induction is used mainly in the USA and is quite spectacular. It consists of confusion, shock and aggression. This can be used on anyone, although in the UK some people don't like this induction and feel threatened at just seeing a demonstration. The subject may 'look' as if they have gone into a faint but they are fully aware and find it pleasant and relaxing. It's quite extraordinary and is very effective, showing the power of suggestion at its best.

People who experience a severe trauma or scare will automatically go into hypnosis. The conscious mind stops processing and the subconscious is vulnerable. (The instant induction needs another person to induce the hypnosis.)

The rapid induction. Dave Elman, a more

modern master of hypnosis, developed what I believe to be the most successful technique of rapid induction. It uses confusion and complicated short instructions to close down the conscious part of the mind, exposing the subconscious. It is very effective and this type of induction is useful for inducing hypnosis when a person has already experienced it before. (This induction needs another to do the hypnosis.)

The progressive induction. This is the most important and simple induction to use. The words guide the subject into hypnosis. Therefore it can be induced via a person, cassette tapes or videos. You don't have to have another person present to guide you into hypnosis, you just listen to a pre-recording, either bought or prepared yourself.

It is simply an exercise in relaxation with many different words to induce reaction and participation. For example, the words may suggest, 'Tighten the muscles in your feet.' The instructions occupy the conscious while relaxing the mind, allowing the suggestion to be accepted. As the instructions become monotonous the mind relaxes even more. It literally bores the person into hypnosis. Because it is more effective to have at least a modicum of attention while inducing the relaxation, it is better to have a script with varied words. It is not as effective to keep using the same verb continuously in the instructions, e.g. '*Tighten* the muscles in your feet, now *relax* those muscles. Now *tighten* the muscles in your calves ... now begin to *relax* the muscles. *Tighten* the muscles in your thighs, now begin to *relax* those long muscles.'

There are exceptions to certain words that may be used continually to join the suggestion together, e.g. *now* and also *deeper* can be used liberally, or powerful words such as *down*, when used repetitively can lead the subject deeper into trance. (This is the only method in which the subject has no need for another person to lead them – it can be taped.)

The progressive relaxation technique gradually slows down the system of the client and so, however stressed or tense they may be at the beginning, eventually this technique will guide them into deep relaxation. The technique ensures a relaxation that is adequate enough to be followed by the appropriate stop-smoking suggestion and as long as the problem isn't trauma-based and is in the subject's interest, the subconscious will accept the new programme.

You can prevent yourself going into hypnosis by refusing to relax, otherwise there is no reason that the suggestion shouldn't work. Don't spend time on worrying whether you are achieving hypnosis – just let your mind drift with the words and it will happen.

First you must accept that you can be hypnotised. That it is nothing to do with intelligence, or will power – it is a fact that we can all hypnotise ourselves. And if you are not attaining it, then it's your responsibility. Like anything else, practice makes perfect. In order to attain effective self-hypnosis, I would suggest that in the beginning a volunteer should guide you with the instructions given. Then, when you have been guided into trance for the first time, it will be much easier for you to do it yourself.

To help you understand the difficulties, I would like you to imagine that you are a native of Barbados and that you are watching television. You have never experienced severe cold or felt snow. There is a film on the TV, showing a group of people stranded in a snowstorm. Their car has broken down and they are suffering from the incredible cold, getting frostbite. Not being prepared or dressed properly they are exposed to the elements. If you had never experienced the cold of a snowstorm, it would be impossible for someone to explain it so that you could actually feel it and experience the extreme cold these people were feeling.

If you were taken to England and experienced a cold day, this would still not give you even a basic insight of what the snow feels like and how cold it can become in a blizzard. If you were taken to Scotland during snow blizzards, you would have a first-hand experience of what this type of cold is like in relation to the cold you had already been subjected to. When you returned to Barbados and a picture came on the television screen of a snowstorm, you would know exactly how it felt, and you may even spontaneously shiver with just the thought of it. Once your mind has experienced a feeling it is permanently stored in the memory banks. Your memory can therefore immediately remind you of such experiences. A favourite song can bring a feeling of sadness or joy or a particular smell can awaken a memory in a split second.

In terms of hypnosis, if you first try it yourself

with just your own meditations or with a selection of the many cassette tapes or videos, you risk not getting anywhere near the true experience, like the Barbadian watching the snow blizzard who has no idea what it feels like to be really cold and cannot figure out what all the fuss is about. If you approach self-hypnosis knowing what to expect, or rather what not to expect, with practice and perseverance there is no reason why you cannot use this incredible control of your own mind to change your attitude and personality defects. It is that powerful.

Also, once you have experienced hypnosis with a helpful guide you can easily attain it by yourself if you have been given some good instructions into hypnosis and methods to help you, such as the instructions in this book.

The reason so many people are disappointed by self-hypnosis tapes or videos is that they expect to feel hypnotised, even to the extent of expecting to be in a coma-like state.

Once you have been hypnotised, the tapes and videos can be very beneficial, although no more so than creating your own tape recordings from something as simple as a pocket recorder and creating your own personal scripts from the rules for suggestions given in Chapters 3 and 4.

There are four methods you can use to attain self-hypnosis. I have listed them below with their advantages and disadvantages. However, without question, for speed and depth it is to your advantage to have someone to help guide you through your first hypnosis experience.

Method one

Use a volunteer to guide you into hypnosis and take you through the method for deep self-hypnosis. The advantages are that the volunteer can use the book and if they follow the instructions carefully they will induce good deep hypnosis. In order to produce a deep trance all you need is suggestion hypnosis. Anyone you feel comfortable with can read the words and you will go into hypnosis.

Disadvantages: The attitude or type of volunteer you have chosen can affect the results you achieve. They may be a giggler or their voice is not particularly relaxing, and choosing an unconfident stutterer would be very distracting.

Method two

Use a tape recording or video to induce self-hypnosis. However, there are so many possible distractions when you are alone, such as the phone ringing or your mind being kept busy with daily routines or dinner plans, that you may find it difficult to relax enough for a good deep trance. If you persevere you will certainly relax.

Disadvantages: You don't have someone to guide you and use deepeners that encourage a much deeper state of trance. You don't have someone there to pace the hypnosis to your individual thoughts. Videos and tapes do not take into account something that may distract you and so you can easily become out of sync with the induction at the beginning stages of hypnosis. Struggling and worrying that you can't catch up interferes with the relaxation and chances of hypnosis so make sure your words are slow and methodic, highlighting certain points that are important to you.

Method three

Use an experienced hypnotherapist to induce hypnosis. The advantages are that the hypnotherapist will have the expertise to sound confident although they will only be following similar scripts illustrated in this book. There is no reason why the volunteer cannot induce the same quality of hypnosis. For suggestion hypnosis only, an experienced hypnotherapist is not a necessity. You can even teach professional suggestion hypnosis in as little as an hour. For advanced techniques, then an experienced hypnotherapist is essential. Not because it is dangerous, because it isn't, but mainly because without the experience it will be difficult for the inexperienced to work efficiently and easily. It is all down to experience and a good training background.

In my workshops I have trained hypnotherapists who have read every book conceivable on the workings of hypnosis, and still did not have the confidence to carry out the advanced techniques to create a change of behaviour in their clients. After the all-important one-to-one training their confidence was established. For a student to try to learn advanced techniques in hypnosis from books alone is like going for a solo flight in a light aircraft without having any previous one-to-one training, or never even having sat in an aircraft before the flight. It can be done, but it takes absolute confidence and guts, and when it comes to the crunch not everyone is cut out for it. Therefore you tend to find a lot of hypnotherapists who stick to suggestion therapy only.

Disadvantages: Using an experienced hypnotherapist for just 'suggestion' hypnosis will cost you anything between £35–£250 per session, and they will only be working with a similar script that can be found in the following chapters. Anyone who can read the appropriate scripts in a confident and easy manner can attain the same level of hypnosis as the professional hypnotherapist, but without the extra cost.

Of the three methods of induction I have outlined, we will be concentrating on the progressive induction. The other two are more advanced techniques and have no extra benefit apart from the time element. The main progressive induction script I have included in this book is the only one I personally use for all my clients in the first session.

Method four

Instruction with groups. These are quite popular

and range from half days to weekend courses. This of course depends on the technique used and the instructions. They are a cheaper option than one-to-one therapy but generally have a much lower success rate – but they still work.

If you decide to practise self-hypnosis without the assistance of an experienced therapist, using a volunteer to do the induction or taping it yourself, the progressive induction is a must. It certainly is the cheapest option with a healthy success rate. I will therefore be concentrating on this particular technique in this book.

3

All hypnosis is self-hypnosis, but generally when people talk about self-hypnosis they are inquiring about how a person puts themselves into hypnosis, without the aid of another to guide them. The hypnotherapist is just the guide that helps the subject into hypnosis.

All relaxation techniques will create a hypnotic state, even if the relaxation procedure never uses the formal name 'hypnosis'. It is normally called just plain 'relaxation'. This slows down the brain waves, which in turn creates the state we know as 'hypnosis'. So if you have been lead into relaxation by tapes or a trainer using relaxation techniques you have already been hypnotised without realising it. If you have been in meditation, or practised yoga, you have been in hypnosis.

The stage hypnotist has developed certain inductions that put a person instantly into hypnosis. The induction takes only seconds, but these techniques are not 100% reliable and generally work for approximately one-third of any audience. The stage hypnotist is particularly experienced in such instant induction techniques because time is of the essence to in the act, and the audience will very quickly get bored and restless if the subject is not rapidly hypnotised. On the other hand, the hypnotherapist has the luxury of time and can choose the induction he or she prefers, whether it be rapid or slow and relaxing. The hypnotherapist is more likely to take the slower approach, considering that he or she will be treating both the susceptible and the not so susceptible subject. Knowing that everyone can be induced into hypnosis, the hypnotherapist would sometimes rather not stand the chance of losing his subject's belief structure at the beginning of therapy with the less successful rapid or instant techniques.

At one time, in the experimental stages of hypnotism that occurred as far back as the 1800s,

James Esdaile, a master at hypnosis treatment, would take up to an hour and a half to induce deep trance for anaesthesia. The modern hypnotherapist, with a little more understanding of how the mind works, has been able to speed up the induction and has a choice of three types of induction, ranging in duration from seconds to minutes, depending on preference.

So, we are dealing with percentages when we talk of induction. The instant induction needs a very confident hypnotist and a suggestible subject. The rapid induction works on a larger percentage of people, while the progressive, slow method is far more reliable as a first induction.

The stage hypnotist will be able to work with approximately 33% of the audience using instant inductions; the competent hypnotherapist can work with 100% of the subjects as long as he or she takes the necessary time each individual will require. Self-hypnosis has a lot of hurdles to get over, which, if not prepared for, prevent some subjects feeling any relaxation at all – from whatever induction they use. Thus, we have to be aware of the obstacles, and an understanding of how the mind works will be of great benefit to the person who finds it difficult to go into hypnosis.

The first major obstacle is that there is no feeling in hypnosis, just as there is no feeling when you go into daydream. So how do you know when you are hypnotised? The fact is that you do not.

You may have seen people who have been hypnotised in a show perform extraordinary tasks while on stage and then, when they are brought out of trance, refuse to believe they were in hypnosis at all. Just like the alcoholic who has to admit he is an alcoholic before he can be treated, the person who is going to practise self-hypnosis needs to accept that it is unlikely that he or she will have any feelings in hypnosis except that of relaxation. The exception is when the subconscious may have taken a suggestion on board from something read earlier or spoken in hypnosis indicating there may be a feeling or tingling sensation that indicates the state of hypnosis. The subject may not have any memory of hearing this information but it presents itself in hypnosis and a tingling sensation may be experienced.

It was common practice for a hypnotist to suggest this to his subject as a suggestibility test. The subjects who said they felt a slight tingling had accepted the suggestion and therefore were suggestible. The people feeling nothing had not accepted the suggestion but could still be experiencing the same quality of hypnosis.

Hypnotising yourself

This chapter has been designed to give you a simple guide on how to hypnotise yourself; alternatively, you could ask a partner or a trusted friend to help. It could be fun. I have listed the instructions and tools for you to do this; the words used in hypnosis are called 'scripts'

1. The induction scripts are the words used to induce a hypnotic trance. The trance is similar to a daydream. You are totally aware of what is happening around you.

2. The suggestion scripts are the words in the form of instructions that are devised to create your desired change, i.e. to stop smoking, which you tag on to the end of the induction.

3. The counting out of hypnosis are the words used to gently ease you out of the deep relaxation. This should be at the end of your suggestion script, after the aversion.

The counting out script is not a necessity but it is a

very nice way to end the trance. Otherwise you can just open your eyes as you wish. Since hypnosis is like a daydream you are always able to end the trance at will. Moreover, it is prudent to remember that you do not need deep relaxation in hypnosis for it to work. That is why some misguided people, who are experiencing a light relaxation, think they are 'not' in hypnosis. The truth is there is no actual feeling in hypnosis, so you can only trust the fact that when you are relaxed your brain waves decrease and that is the state of hypnosis. As soon as you use your imagination you are in hypnosis, and all the induction scripts are created precisely to encourage you to imagine.

If you have had any form of relaxation therapy or used a relaxation tape, you will have experienced a form of hypnosis, even if you were unaware of it at the time. Since there is no feeling in hypnosis, you do not even have to be relaxed to experience it; in fact you can be in a state of deep shock. You just have to accept that when your brain waves are reduced causing you to drift into a daydream you are sufficiently relaxed to accept suggestions. On the other hand, if you experience a deep relaxation, a wonderful sinking or even tingling sensation, then you are highly suggestable. Either way you have the same chance of accepting the suggestions or instructions that are the essence of the therapy.

The instructions change the attitude, which in turn changes the behaviour. The depth in trance does not ensure the suggestion works, it only serves as a pleasant feeling to be deeply relaxed. You have just as much chance of accepting suggestions in a light trance as in a deep trance. To say you are not deep enough in trance for the suggestion to work is like saying that someone was 'a little bit pregnant'. You are either in hypnosis or not.

I, personally, have never felt anything in hypnosis, although the changes in my behaviour have been immediate and permanent.

A LITTLE KNOWLEDGE OF INDUCTION

The induction is a method of inducing hypnosis. There are three basic ways to induce hypnosis:

1. Shock: a fright can induce shock, which in itself creates a hypnotic trance. The conscious crashes like a computer when it is overloaded. It is not dangerous or unpleasant, simply a fact.

2. Confusion: created by overloading the mind so that it closes down. Approximately three easy

instructions that are a play on words, and so cause confusion, in turn creates a conscious shutdown.

3. Boredom: a long 'script' of calming words creating a trance, or daydream state.

For self-hypnosis, boredom is the most successful method of inducing hypnosis. The compilation of words massage the mind into relaxation. The resulting calmness slows the brain waves down and allows the subconscious or inner mind to come forward as a means of self-preservation, to protect you while you are relaxing. Hypnosis is therefore a heightened state of awareness and not sleep, which it is often confused with.

CHECK-LIST STEPS FOR SELF-HYPNOSIS

1. *Induction script* – the progressive relaxation.

2. *The main stop-smoking suggestion* – use the main script and later add your own additional words, depending upon your personality or situation.

3. *Counting out script* – facilitates you coming out of hypnosis.

Induction Script

I prefer to use the following progressive induction in the beginning. Later you can choose from the alternatives outlined in the next chapter, or make up your own script following the examples given.

I have also provided a selection of suggestion scripts for stopping smoking in the next chapter, which enable you to adjust the main script. But again I advise you to use the main script, as it is, for the first time. In order to compound the suggestions you can then add remarks from the other stop-smoking suggestions.

You may feel that you prefer to hypnotise yourself every day for three weeks or you may feel that once is enough. Do not be surprised if you just do not want to smoke after the first hypnosis suggestion. If you have a definite and immediate behaviour change – that is, a lack of desire to smoke – then there is no need to follow it up with more.

When taping your voice, you need to be slow and monotonous, talking very slowly and distinctly. It is useful to highlight important words or phrases with voice tone. If you have a volunteer to hypnotise you then they need to speak with a monotonous, gentle voice, but not so exaggeratedly as you would on the cassette tape.

The progressive relaxation

You can choose scripts that take you by the sea, in a garden, on a boat, or on a magical journey. The list is endless but a small percentage of people have a fear of drowning and, therefore, would not find the water very relaxing. I find that the theme of a garden satisfies everyone.

To help you read the script aloud with the correct pauses, I have deliberately exaggerated the spacing between the phrases. It is also important to realise that the grammar does not always have to be precise and words not accurately arranged are not only acceptable, but actually to your advantage, as this causes a controlled confusion of the mind. Chapter 4 has some alternative induction scripts that you can choose from as a change.

Progressive relaxation induction script

I want you to imagine that you're checking your body to ensure you become totally relaxed... as your muscles relax... just let your mind relax also... begin with your feet... feel your toes... stretch them... feel the texture of what your feet are resting on... begin to tighten your calves... now relax them... let that relaxation spread past your ankles... up your calves to the back of your knee... feel those muscles easing... resting comfortably... now your thighs... pull them tight... be aware of those long muscles tensing... now relax those muscles... feel them lengthening and resting comfortably... feel your legs as they sink even deeper into the cushions as you relax even more... now your stomach muscles... pull them together gently... now let them expand and relax comfortably.

Your shoulders and back muscles... flex your shoulders... feel those muscles pull across your back... now let your shoulders slouch as you relax the muscles... and notice how your spine sinks deeper into your chair, as you relax even more deeply... notice how easy and regular your breathing has become... Now your fingertips... and fingers... clench them... feel that tension... now relax them... and allow the relaxation to spread up your arms to your neck... Make sure your neck is comfortable, with your head in an easy position... tighten up your neck muscles... now let them loosen up... as the muscles relax allow your neck to shrink into a comfortable position.

Your face muscles are flat and stretch comfortably across your face... squeeze up your face... and feel the tension... now relax those muscles and feel them lengthening... and softening... relaxing... more than ever before.

You can now feel the air temperature against your skin... It feels smooth and comfortable... now you can allow the relaxation to spread to your scalp... knowing that you are relaxed throughout your body... from the top of your head ... to the tips of your toes.

Your body is now loose... and limp... and heavy... and relaxed... notice how your body is sinking deeper into relaxation... as your breathing becomes more regular and easy... in a moment I will count slowly from one... to ten... and with each number you drift... deeper... and deeper... into peaceful relaxation... one... two... three... four... five... six... seven... eight... nine... ten. (Count slowly and deliberately.)

You are now feeling so deeply relaxed... you find it easy to focus your attention... and imagine things very clearly... and I want you to imagine that you are standing on a balcony... which has steps leading down to a beautiful garden... as you look into the garden... you see that it is surrounded with lovely trees... ensuring the garden is private... secluded and peaceful... There are flower beds... set in the lovely lawn... and further along is a waterfall... flowing into a stream... Listen to the sound of the water... as you look around... you see the trees... and you hear a faint sound of a bird in the distance... adding to the feeling of deep... relaxation... through your entire being... If you look more closely you will see that there are five steps leading down to the garden... and then a small path... that leads to the waterfall... in a moment we will walk down the steps... and with each step you go deeper... and deeper into relaxation... So let's begin.

Watch your foot as you place it on to the first step... and as you do this you feel yourself going deeper into relaxation.

Down on to the second step... and as you feel your foot firmly placed on the step... you feel a wonderful relief... as you drift even deeper into relaxation... down on to the third step... feeling wonderfully free and... so... so... relaxed... as your foot reaches for the fourth step... another wave of relaxation drifts through your whole body... down on to the fifth step now... and feeling even more deeply relaxed than ever before.

Now you are standing on the lawn... you see a little way ahead... is a waterfall... and at the side of it is a garden bench... notice the colour of the bench... what it is made of.

In a moment I would like you to walk over to the bench... and sit down on the bench... When you sit

*down you will be surprised at how comfortable it is...
and then you will be even more relaxed than you are
now... so let's begin to walk over... now sit down on the
bench... and as you sit down on the bench... take a
deep breath... and as you breathe out... you feel a wave
of relaxation go through your body... relaxing every
muscle and nerve... as you breathe in... you breathe in
positive thoughts... and as you breathe out... you
breathe out negative thoughts... leaving room for
more positive thoughts.*

Pre-stop-smoking suggestion
The following paragraph should be included in
between the induction script and the stop-smoking
script, as a pre-suggestion.

*In this deep and special relaxation... your subconscious
mind... for your own protection, takes note of what is
happening around you... So these suggestions, which
are for your benefit... go directly to your subconscious
mind... There they are accepted... because these ideas
are for your benefit... These thoughts become firmly
fixed deep in your inner mind... Embedded, so they
remain with you, long after I have you open your
eyes... Helping your being to change those things you*

want to change, for your own sake.

The main stop-smoking script

This main script has been used, and only slightly altered, for years and has been the basis of the *Stop Smoking In One Hour* programme.

You have now made one of the most important decisions of your life... to save your life... by giving up smoking... giving up polluting your lungs... your lungs perform one of the most important functions in your body... without them you cannot breathe... you cannot live... it is essential for you to keep your lungs clean and fill them with fresh air... so you can live... and be healthy.

Your body has to cope with pollution from the air that you breathe... your lungs are adaptable and can cope with this... but the extra strain that smoking brings about... the extra concentrated pollution you are sucking in from each cigarette... is weakening your insides... your mouth... your throat... your lungs... your stomach, and your blood... are just a few of the victims of your carelessness... but also the dangerous chemicals that are used in the pesticides sprayed on the tobacco as it grows are used to kill insects... and now are slowly killing you... you have been forcing people around you... even young children... to breathe in your extra pollution... you have been ignorant to how unsociable it has become... no more... now you care about yourself and the people around you.

From now on... you will find that you are more and more conscious... that smoking is bad for you... you are more and more aware... of the damage it is doing to your health... that it is increasing... by many times your chances of dying... a horrible and painful death... from cancer or heart disease... you imagine yourself fighting and struggling for breath... or suffering with severe damage to your limbs and arteries.

You may fool yourself ... that this... is a long way off... but you know it may... catch up with you eventually... if you carry on smoking... you know that smoking is doing serious damage... to your limbs and arteries.

You may fool yourself... that this... is a long way off... but you know it will catch up with you eventually... you know that smoking is doing serious damage to your general level of fitness... you hate the unpleasant taste in your mouth and throat... you hate the way that smoke makes your hair and clothes smell... especially when you know that other people around you... are noticing it too... so many people have been able to give up now... and they notice it more when you smell of smoke... even being beside you makes their own clothes smell.

You know how much smoking is costing you and how much better you can spend the money on other things... you know that deep down you are lying to yourself... when you tell yourself that smoking calms and relaxes you... it's only a crutch – you can cope easily without it... you know it is really only making you more tense... it is no longer sociable, in fact the smoker is now a misfit... a danger to non-smokers... forcing them to become passive smokers... against their will.

You find the thought of a cigarette... so disgusting... that you do not want to even pick one up... from now on you cut off any urge to have a cigarette... before it even strikes you... by relaxing ... and slowing down your breathing... as you do this the urge to smoke... disappears... your subconscious is finding ways to get rid of your smoking habit... redirecting the satisfaction... to a good habit... more advantageous to you... you have no desire at all from now on to smoke... your craving has gone... for ever.

The whole idea of smoking is offensive to you...

you just don't need it any more... your inner mind finds safe and effective ways to rid yourself of this... revolting habit... and as your complete mastery... over your former smoking habit increases... you become proud of your self-control and willpower... your lungs and throat... feel so much clearer... you have much more energy... you feel so much more relaxed... even food tastes so much better... and you enjoy it so much more... although you find your appetite doesn't increase... you feel more like eating healthy foods... and so you find you are able to maintain your desired weight much more easily... while protecting your body... from the poison of further smoking... your inner mind automatically balancing your food intake... to keep you fit and healthy... your resistance to illness and disease increases steadily day by day... now just take a deep breath... and relax... now take a deep breath... and relax.

You can now terminate the trance with the counting out of hypnosis script or you can increase the effectiveness of the stop-smoking suggestions by using the aversion therapy script. I always utilise the aversion script as it adds to the overall effect of the stop-smoking programme.

Counting out of hypnosis

To bring yourself out of hypnosis you can count backwards from ten to one. Decreasing the numbers gives the suggestion of coming 'up' out of hypnosis. The reverse is also true – counting 'down' gives the suggestion of going deeper.

In a moment, I am going to count from ten to one... and at the count of one you feel fully aware, fully alert and your eyes will open... ten... nine... eight coming up now... seven... six... five... more and more alert... four... three... two... one, eyes open.

AVERSION THERAPY

The aversion therapy is a suggestion that helps the mind to experience the unpleasant side of cigarettes that is in denial from the left side of the brain. It can also implant a negative reaction to cigarettes, helping the smoker to stop more easily. Aversion therapies can also take the form of a suggestion that the cigarette tastes of rubber – or something equally offensive – and when you return to a normal state, the thought of a cigarette repulses you by reminding you of the rubber. This helps you stop and when the suggestion has worn off it has given you that all-important time to realise that you don't need a cigarette. The aversion used here does not use rubber but it is equally effective. It can be read, or placed on your tape, after the induction and main suggestion for stopping smoking.

I want you to imagine you are going to walk into a room... A familiar room... The room has a table and a chair... The table can be a coffee table... a dining room table... or even a desk... any table at all... That can be at home or work.

Now I want you to imagine in your mind's eye... that you are walking into the room... close the door... Go over to the chair... sit down on that chair... and on the table in front of you... I want you to place all the cigarettes you have ever smoked in your life... on that table... Watch the pile getting higher and higher... Some cigarettes are spilling over... (take a moment to allow the focus)*... Now I want you to put one of those cigarettes from that pile in your mouth... And I want you to simultaneously light the cigarette in your mouth... as well as all the cigarettes on the table... and watch that smoke billowing around... Getting thicker... and thicker... going into your hair and your clothes...*

Some of the tar goes down the side of your chin... you try to wipe it off with the back of your hand... It just sticks to the back of your hand... And all the time the smoke is getting thicker... and thicker... it's all around you now... getting thicker... What's the room like now?

Let that picture fade and come out of the room... In a moment I want you to go back into that room... but before you do... I want you to clean it up... you can do it any way you like... Open the windows... get a set of cleaners in... redecorate it... but make sure it's clear.

Now I want you to walk back in that room... You don't have to close the door behind you... Go to that chair... Sit on that chair.. and on the table in front of you... which is now empty... I want you to place all the cigarettes you are going to smoke from now on... and note how many are left on the table... If there are any left I want you to find a way to get rid of them... you can destroy them... or smoke them now... but you must make sure there are none left. Take a moment to do this (allowing 30 seconds' silence)... and when you have finished... you can just allow yourself to relax even more... Now take a deep breath in and allow yourself to feel that wave of relaxation float through you as you release your breath slowly and rhythmically... breathing out negative thoughts and *filling the space by breathing in positive thoughts and energy.*

The following scripts are examples of further suggestions for stopping smoking. They should be used in addition to the main script, as required, and not used to replace it. They give you the choice of a mix-and-match patchwork of words to help create your own personal suggestions to suit your own personality and situation.

Breaking the smoking links

You have broken all the links that placed smoking in your everyday activities... You cannot imagine any activity you would ever do that now includes smoking... it seems completely out of place... Those activities you enjoy would only be ruined by the presence of a cigarette... You wouldn't want to do anything that stopped you from enjoying feeling good about yourself... breathing beautiful fresh air... concentrating fully on life... tasting, smelling and feeling everything that can be possibly experienced... All the things you have been denying yourself all this time and you can now can enjoy for the rest of your life.

A new and exciting life

You have now started a new and exciting life... A life that promises to be more pleasurable... much more satisfying... giving you so much more joy... Now that you have removed smoking from your life completely... you find every aspect of your life improving... Your concentration is greater... your health is improved... your confidence is stronger and cannot be wavered... your energy and vitality increases... as your body relishes the new supply of oxygen... you feel a sense of freedom inside... The air surprises you with its freshness... flowing into your lungs easily... revitalising your body with each new breath... And with every day that passes... as a permanent, confident non-smoker... every aspect of your life improves.

For the social drinker

Now you can enjoy an alcoholic drink without the handicap of holding an unpleasant appendage... You find that smoking just spoils your taste... interferes with your taste buds... You look more calm... and confident... as you are able to be proud... proud that you have managed to get rid of the smoking habit...

You find that you enjoy your life more with your new-found freedom... and feel free... Free to go to the homes of friends who are non-smokers... and enjoy the evening... without making excuses to go outside the room to smoke... or not even being able to accept the invitation... It allows you freedom in both business and social situations not having to worry if you are upsetting a non-smoker by smoking... because why should you be polluting their air with your unpleasant and offensive smoking habit... no more. You are happy to visit restaurants that are smoke free, and enjoy taking that extra time you can now spend... instead of having to rush to have a cigarette. You wonder why you needed to in the first place... You feel so delightfully free and healthy... especially at the prospect of your healthy future.

For the social drinker II

Allow yourself to feel comfortable and relaxed... and you imagine yourself in a social setting... You are completely self-assured and confident, making conversation easily... meeting people without requiring any unnecessary actions at all... Because you have no urge to smoke... there is no compulsion to have a cigarette... You don't even think about having a cigarette... the thought never even occurs to you... No one can tempt you to smoke... as you have no desire at all to even hold one in your hand... If someone tries to offer you a cigarette you are surprised they would even think of doing so... and being a confirmed non-smoker you firmly refuse... confidently and proudly...

You notice the excessive hand movements and nervous gestures of the smokers around you... seeing how uneasy they look... you realise that you look confident... and content... as a proud and satisfied non-smoker... enjoying the freedom of being able to go into any public place and not have to worry if it is non-smoking or if you are objectionable to a non-smoker around you... you are now free... not having to be irritated at not being able to light your cigarette because you have mislaid your lighter or matches... you notice how tense smokers are when they need to buy a packet of cigarettes and they cannot get served... and how ridiculous they look. You are aware of the smell of the smoke on their clothing... and their breath. You are acutely aware of the cigarette smell... and are amazed that you could have smoked in the past... although you are aware of it... other people smoking is their choice and you are pleased it is no longer your choice to smoke... This awareness only *strengthens your decision to be the non-smoker... in fact the thought just doesn't occur to you at all in any situation.*

An option for a female

You are strong, self-assured, confident... Your sense of well-being increases with every day... as your commitment to not smoking increases... You will feel vital and full of energy... as you carry out the decision to be a non-smoker... You will simply no longer desire cigarettes... whenever you are offered a cigarette you refuse without effort... it will be an unconscious reaction... and with each refusal you will become more confident and self-assured... knowing that you have the power within you to stop smoking... and knowing that it is so easy... even easier than you had originally thought. You already know that no habit is stronger than the power of your mind... which created the habit in the first place... and you know too that you can use your mind to beat the tobacco as many people have before... You feel energised... and revitalised... as your body no longer has to deal with the toxins... and pollutants... you used to put into it...

You take a moment to imagine yourself in ten or twenty years' time on an imaginary television screen you bring forward in your mind... Look closely at your face... wrinkled with smoking and an unhealthy pallor... Now, on a second screen at the side of the first set... imagine that this is the same face but that you have not smoked and look to see how much less lined you are... more healthy you look... and your breathing comfortable... You're able to concentrate more easily on tasks at hand... and you find that you are more alert... and capable of handling any situation that arises... Allow the good picture of you as a non-smoker to fill your view and allow the old image of the smoker to be obliterated, just leaving the main television filling your vision... a happy... comfortable... picture... knowing the old smoker picture is safely in the past... no longer restricting you... you are now free to enjoy life.

You have a heightened sense of purpose and satisfaction as you realise how much money you are saving as a non-smoker... not only money saved from the fact you no longer need to purchase cigarettes, but money saved on doctors' fees... and insurance policies... With this knowledge you have a new-found sense of freedom and independence... you are no longer tied to a dirty habit that is so dangerous to your health... a habit that is destroying your body... and it's *so easy... you will feel less constricted in the options you have... You are more comfortable with yourself as you realise that you have made the right decision... the decision to be a non-smoker... and proud of your achievement.*

Smoking script – feminine

You are a beautiful... self-confident... elegant person. You have an innate ability to carry yourself with purpose and poise... you do not make any unnecessary actions... You have absolutely no desire or urge to have a cigarette... the thought never enters your mind... Because you know smoking is an unconscious habit... you are immediately aware that your hands are completely relaxed and have no need to be constantly occupied... showing your weakness... instead of hiding it... The confidence you attained from being a smoker is now in your mental software... your memory... so you no longer need the cigarette... it is out of date... an old programme... This knowledge only relaxes you more... and more... you allow yourself to enjoy this feeling of relaxation, knowing you do not have to perform any unnecessary acts to fill the time... As you relax you feel the little stresses that normally would have affected you just flow away... leaving you even more calm and self-confident... You find that situations become easier to resolve as you can fully concentrate on them without the distraction of unconscious habits... You have no desire to smoke... when you watch other people smoke... In fact... you find yourself noticing the unpleasant smell ... and the dirty ashtrays ... that surround those who smoke... The more you notice these... the more your commitment to not smoking increases... and you realise how happy you are.

You begin to notice how clean and fresh your own clothes smell... and how clean your breath is... The air tastes fresher, crisper and cleaner... With every breath you take you enjoy the full taste of unpolluted cigarette air... As you breathe in you are filled with positive thoughts... and with every breath out you release any nervousness and tension.

You begin to really enjoy the marvellous taste of food... Your body savours the taste of each bite... getting more out of every mouthful... increasing your satisfaction and revitalising your body... Your body is now more tuned to how much food it requires... and can automatically tell when it has had sufficient for its needs... Allowing you to easily stop overeating... knowing that you have all the sustenance you require... leaving you contented... satisfied and happy.

Smoking script – masculine

You are strong, self-assured confident... Your sense of well-being increases with every day as your commitment to not smoking increases... You will feel vital and full of energy as you carry out the decision to be a non-smoker... You will simply no longer desire cigarettes... whenever you are offered a cigarette you will refuse without effort... it will be an unconscious reaction... and with each refusal you will become more confident and self-assured... knowing that you have the power within you to stop smoking... and knowing that it is so easy... even easier than you had originally thought... You already know that no habit is stronger than the power of your mind that created the habit in the first place... and you know too that you can use your mind to beat the tobacco... for you have a very strong mind... You feel energised and revitalised as your body no longer has to deal with the toxins and pollutants you used to put into it. You're able to concentrate more easily on tasks at hand, and you find that you are more alert, and capable of handling any situation that arises.

You have a heightened sense of purpose and satisfaction as you realise how much money you are saving as a non-smoker... not only money saved from the fact you no longer need to purchase cigarettes, but money saved on doctors' fees, and insurance policies. With this knowledge you have a new-found sense of freedom and independence... you are no longer tied to a dirty habit that is so dangerous to your health... a habit that is destroying your body... and it's so easy... you will feel less constricted in the options you have. You are more comfortable with yourself as you realise that you have made the right decision... the decision to be a non-smoker. You keep a record of your progress as a non-smoker... day by day, week by week... you are successful... and proud of your achievement.

The TV screen technique

This is another successful technique that you can add to the end of the aversion, just before you give the instructions to end the trance. It uses a television screen to create your new blueprint for your subconscious/inner mind to follow. Remember, imagination is the language of your subconscious. I always end my therapy with this method.

Picture yourself on a very large TV set, about 3 metres high, exactly how you do 'not' want to be as an unfortunate smoker... your body being sabotaged by the poison you are putting in it.

On the right-hand corner of the TV screen, project an image of you exactly how you DO wish and want yourself to be... healthy... fit... confident... as a satisfied non-smoker... (add your own suggestions here to reinforce the effectiveness. Remember, it is your imagination and you are in control.)... *Notice what you are wearing... how good you look... how good you feel.*

Now swish the good picture across the screen so that it completely fills the screen and totally obliterates the old picture.

You will notice that there are some dials at the bottom of the screen... These are special dials... positive emotional dials... If you adjust them they will adjust the picture with the emotions you desire... So start to adjust the dials... notice your confidence more balanced... improved health... (add exactly what you want here)... *adjust the dials until the picture is exactly right for you... Now let that picture fade.*

Now bring back the old picture... looks even worse now, doesn't it? Just notice how differently you feel about it.

Now bring the good picture up on to the right-

hand corner of the screen again. And do what you did before... but twice... swish the new picture across the screen so that the old picture is completely destroyed and the new picture totally fills the screen.

Stop smoking with hypnosleep – a powerful but short suggestion

At the beginning of the tape you record a few words to check your voice level – to make sure it is not too loud and that you keep the same voice level when you speak the suggestion at the end of the tape. 'And now to sleep' should be at the beginning of the tape. Remember, don't speak too loudly. Use gentle and quietly soothing words, loud enough for you to hear but not so loud that they will wake you up. Then leave a gap until the end of the recording (allowing about three minutes to talk in the suggestion). The gap is so that you can go to sleep undisturbed.

The suggestion at the end should be played when you are actually asleep. The first part of the tape, after the words 'and now to sleep', should be blank, to allow you to sleep.

If it takes you longer than the 40 minutes to fall asleep, then use a timer. Set it for about 3.30 am, or when you know you will be sleeping. You can buy one from an electrical shop. You need to say the following words before the suggestion (at the end of the tape); this brings you the depth you need. Then follow it with the main suggestion below.

You can hear me but you won't wake up
You can hear me but you won't wake up
You can hear me but you won't wake up.

You have been smoking for too long... any time you put poison into your system... you weaken it... Before... you may not have realised what damage it has been doing... to your system... you were only aware of the side effects... Your body has been telling you for so long... little tell-tale signs... shortage of breath... worry about the effects... little niggly remarks in your mind... your inner mind trying to communicate... At last you have got the message... no more... no more poisoning... no more damage... your body is getting mature now... and it needs all the energy... you have... So much energy is used up with fighting the pollution... you cannot help... already in the air... where you work... where you live... that it now needs help from you... help... only you can give to yourself... to stop smoking... your inner mind will then be able to make sure that your body heals... re-energising the damage... to strengthen and heal...

Any chemical addiction is easily dealt with... it is cleared by your subconscious... If you have smoked because of a trauma... your subconscious can now work on that area... and fix it... then place it into the past... as an important learning period of your life... you can now look forward to the wonderful... healthy future... You no longer have any need to smoke... Any time you see a cigarette... you see it... how it is... a poison, and you know it's not glamorous... or sophisticated... but just a bad... immature... unsociable habit.

A habit you no longer want... or need... You are now about to join the world of the healthy... no longer an outcast... looking after your body... making sure you have quality in your life... at the time... you feel so free now... so happy... so much more healthy.

You eat healthily... and wisely... and always what your body needs... and no more... Your body is very important to you, so you feed it with respect... and you enjoy healthy food... and you enjoy new control... control over what you want and desire.

It is better if you keep to the words in the above suggestions, as they have been proven to have a very good impact. The mind massage allows you to sleep comfortably.

With both sleep and suggestion hypnosis it may work immediately, or you may feel more comfortable hypnotising yourself daily for up to three weeks. It really depends upon your behaviour. If you do not want a cigarette then you need not continue; if you are not sure then continue.

Keep your book handy and if you feel you want a cigarette in the future, just reinforce yourself with a top-up. However, once someone has stopped even by willpower alone, it is generally permanent.

4

MIND RELAXERS
&
DE-STRESS SCRIPTS

I have devoted this chapter to some very pleasant stress relief relaxation techniques – a very graceful way to induce hypnotic trance. They are mind fantasy inductions in which the words gently massage you into a luxuriously calm mind, giving you that well-needed break from what might be a stressful period. They are a pleasant guide into trance and very useful for relaxation.

This type of induction works for both the visual and the not-so-visual person. However, the visual person – i.e. the person who can imagine places and scenes very clearly in their mind, like a picture – will find it much easier. For the non-visual person the script in chapter 3 is more direct and may be easier for you to follow. The purpose of this book is to give you the choices that make hypnosis a wonderful experience.

These relaxation scripts have been designed and created by individuals that I have trained to be hypnotherapists on my advanced hypnotherapy training courses. I hold these courses in the UK, and at several exotic locations around the world as part of my Learning in Paradise programme.

Choosing a script is like choosing food, or furniture – it is a matter of individual taste. As the old saying has it, 'You can't please all of the people all of the time.' I have included a selection so that you can pick and choose the ones that match your personality and specific needs. You can use the one you like, mix and match, or simply create your own by using the given examples to compound your stop-smoking suggestions by repetition.

A little test to see how visual you are

To check whether you are visual or not, close your eyes and think of a house. Look at what colour it is and what it is made of and how it is constructed, then open your eyes. If you *saw* the house as a picture in your mind then you are visual; if you simply *know* what it looks like then you are non-visual. You may even be somwhere in between – that is just how your mind works. It is just your way of using your imagination but if you are non-visual it is less restful to struggle with descriptive words. When you are in hypnosis and hear the words 'see' or 'imagine' just do this as you did with the house. Don't expect flashing lights or vivid pictures, although some people experience such sensations; personally I am non-visual and do not. Hypnosis works just as well whether you are visual or not.

JOURNEY INTO IMAGINATION

Imagine yourself lying under a large beautiful tree in the beautiful garden... you can see the majesty of how it drapes over the greenery surrounding you... Your body is cushioned by the soft moss beneath you... You can feel the warmth of the sun on your legs... your back... your arms.. and your face... The leaves gently swish away in the breeze... creating dancing patterns of light around you... You feel relaxed and content... The only sounds you hear are the soft humming insects and the cheerfully chattering birds in the distance... and the sound of someone calling your name... a voice somewhere in the garden.. A warm... soothing... inviting voice... You sit up and decide to go for a walk... curious about where this beautiful voice is coming from.

From the grassy knoll where you have been resting... you see the most beautiful sight... tall trees... lush and majestic... creating a natural circular surrounding border in your garden... You feel safe and secure.

You see a path gently curving between the masses at brightly coloured flowers... and shrubs... and decide to follow it... As you walk down the path... you notice a hill and as you walk comfortably down the incline... you find you are going deeper and deeper into relaxation... you feel a wonderful feeling of calm as you experience the beauty of the garden you have created... You savour the feeling of the soft grass beneath your feet... and when you come to the path itself... you see that it is made from stones that you have never seen before... princely white and sparkling gold flecks run through the stones...

You anticipate that it will be cold to walk upon... but to your surprise it is warm and as smooth as satin... As you walk... the flowers on either side of the path become taller... and taller... and more exotic...

every colour imaginable... some colours you haven't seen or dreamt of before... And the smell is so delicate and pleasing ... it reminds you of your favourite flowers but subtly different.

Up ahead you see a pond surrounded by rocks and overhanging plants... You hear a gentle splash and an iridescent blue frog jumps into the water... and disappears into the distance... To cross the pond you walk upon the giant lily-pads.

Stopping half way to peer into the clear... clean... water... to look at the brightly coloured fish darting in... and out... of the lily stems... When you reach the other side... you see a set of steps cut into the hill... covered with lush grass... You make your way to the steps... slowly, comfortably... and as you walk down the steps... the voice becomes clearer... and clearer... stronger... and stronger... The steps lead into a cave... as you walk into the cave it leads you into a tunnel made up of pink and yellow rose bushes... the smell overwhelmingly beautiful.

As you emerge you come to a secret place where the trees and foliage form a large cavern... filled with warm glowing blue fluorescent light... Sitting in the middle on a large chair made from crystal is a beautiful lady... her golden hair reaches past her knees... She wears a simple white tunic edged with gold and purple... her face is strong... gentle and wise... she is silent but you are able to see the beauty of life in her presence... and the wonder of the universe and understand that you no longer want to hinder yourself with negativity... you now realise you can take time... to come to this special place and dream... and look to your future... a future where you take care of your body and yourself... You now take a moment to reflect on the wonderful sights and sounds you have experienced or just enjoy a special quiet.

A BEACH FANTASY

Allow yourself to imagine you are lying on a large beach towel... It is the height of summer... and you are lying on soft luxurious golden sands... in the middle of a beautiful beach... You can feel the infinite fineness of the sand below ... moving to accommodate you into the most comfortable position you can imagine... While you lie there feeling totally relaxed... soaking up the strong beating sun... like liquid gold through your pores... you look around at the majestic scenery around you... The beach stretches out to the horizon in a gentle curve... the water laps gently at its edges... Gliding up the foreshore and gliding back out... in tune with your peaceful breathing. With each breath you watch the lapping waves... and feel doubly more relaxed... Heat shimmers off the golden sand... the only life you notice is an exotic sandpiper making its way across its sandy desert... You notice far down the beach the flash as something catches the sun... Curious... you gently rise and make your way down the beach... Your feet sink deeply into the warm sand... with every step only increasing your sense of well-being and relaxation.

You head towards the top of the beach where sand dunes form tiny hills like scale mountains... As you wind between the wind-swept dunes... you notice the vegetation... and the sparse tundras turn to carpets of buffalo grass which in turn become interspersed with sculptured shrubs... looking like miniature bonsai... laid out by an ancient Japanese gardener... As you rise above a crest... trees start to come into view... lining the valley walls with a thick green suit... gnarled trunks form impossible contortions... creating the impression of a frenzied dance... that was captured at its peak... The overhanging canopies of fervent green leaves... cast shimmering patterns of speckled sunlight as you pass into the cool shadows... heading down an old worn path... The path looks disused... as the underbrush has started to tentatively encroach upon it... You are filled with peace and calm... as you continue deeper into the valley... Native plants become more numerous... ferns stretch from the ground... and moss climbs laboriously up the trunks of nearby trees... Pleasant sounds start to insinuate themselves into your consciousness.

Insects hum happily... and a pair of tiny birds shrill sweetly as they dart between the branches of the nearest tree... You notice that the trees are wide and as you walk among them you enjoy the comfortable sensation of being perfectly at home... as these trees have been for centuries... The air seems fresh and moist... and you hear the distant sound of trickling water... You feel totally secure as you wander along the track taking time to smell the multitude of smells that drift past your nose... taking in the thousands of varieties of fauna that seem to crowd around you each species seeming to clamber to be looked at... and examined and cared for.

As you walk... you begin to hear the sound of water increasing... a pleasant rhythmic pounding...

that relaxes you with each step you take... closer and closer... You round a corner and peer between two fronds at a magnificent sight... There in front of you rising high above you, so that you can't see its top is a gigantic waterfall... Seven cascades of water plummet downward into a perfectly circular rock pool at your feet... The sound fills your ears and vibrates gently through your body... sending wave after wave of relaxation... as you stand there feasting on the view... The water is absolutely clear... allowing you to see its smooth rocky bottom... Its lichen-covered surface forming a natural bowl... As you look at the rocks behind the foaming water... you see the glistening surface speckled with bright gold flecks... and realise what you had noticed flashing in the sun earlier... The water is cool and inviting so you move slowly in to the rock pool... feeling the water rise past your feet and up your ankles... cooling and numbing your skin gently... so that you hardly feel them at all... As you move deeper... the pleasant numbness spreads up your arms, legs and over your waist... You allow yourself to drift into the water... floating on your back all of your body resting as you drift in the water... You lie there so... so... comfortable... Completely relaxed...

just enjoying the sense of well-being... and peace... that flows through you... as you drift along.

21ST CENTURY RELAXATION

Out of the warm... comfortable... relaxing shade comes a deep and soft rhythmic drumming... It widens your awareness and you feel your eyes deeply relaxing... you are floating on a cushion of air, perfectly relaxed and centred... Soft white light filters through large diffuse screens that cover all the walls surrounding you... You allow yourself to drift upright... finding yourself standing firmly on the spongy turquoise floor... A soft, rhythmic chanting continues in the background, maintaining a feeling of quiet relaxed calm within you... As you glide your hand over the wall next to you... a section of the screen slides aside revealing a large metallic cylinder... You step inside and gesture downwards... You hardly notice as the floor beneath you sinks softly down... except as a wave of pleasurable relaxation passes over you... The lift stops at an aquamarine panel that opens in front of you... You see ahead of you a translucent chamber filled with pastel vapours... that swirl languidly round the inside... Taking a long, slow, deep breath you step inside the chamber.

As you step inside... you feel your weight seem to fall off you as you become weightless... floating gently in the vapours... surrounding you with their soft colours, soothing your eyes... The vapours start to coalesce around your body... becoming harder and softer in waves that knead you from head to toe... each wave sending your body deeper and deeper into a peaceful relaxation... When every inch of your body has been thoroughly massaged... the vapour becomes a warm liquid flowing slowly over you like liquid mercury... your skin tingles wherever it flows... feeling cleansed and toned... it revitalises every pore and sends undulating messages of tranquillity.

With a sigh of satisfaction you step from the chamber... and walk through two panels that instantly dry your skin as you pass... Slipping into a suit that clings to every contour of your body... you enter the lift and gesture downwards again... The lift sinks down easing you ever more deeply into peacefulness... stopping at a light blue panel that reveals a warm circular enclosure... encased in thick woollen carpet... At the centre of the room a soft red recliner beckons you towards it... and as you seat yourself the light dims automatically, surrounding you in calming yellow light.

The walls and ceiling fade to darkness and a fantastic panoramic view starts to emerge above you... As you let yourself relax totally the chair settles you into a horizontal repose... The scene around you shows vast rustic canyons catching the last rays of a golden sunset... while above you the stars slowly brighten and sparkle... Your eyes focus on a small star directly above you that seems to grow brighter and larger. The canyons fade from view as your whole body flows towards the bright light... Large planetary shapes glide past revolving, slowly revealing multi-coloured patterns... and ever-shifting shapes. The bright light becomes a shining star that advances towards you, growing larger and larger until... you can see solar flares dancing in intricate movements across its surface.

In this stillness you drift towards a huge planet that emerges from behind the star... Its surface ripples with waves of light... and you feel yourself soaring into its atmosphere... A warm calming sense of well-being envelops you from head to toe... as you sink into a soothing flux of prismatic colours... The colours constantly evolve into ordered arrangements that saturate your senses... you float deeper into the effervescent atmosphere... feeling more relaxed the deeper you go. Emerging from the clouds of light... you soar above the planet's surface marvelling... at the intricate patterns of mountainous terrain... Bright pinpoints of light... are dotted at intervals across the horizon... linked with a fibrous net of delicate lines... in primary colours of red and blue... You pass huge lakes of luminous blue... and rocky peaks that pierce the clouds above... Huge herds of fast-moving animals... move rapidly over yellow plains like the shadow of an ancient dragon, flying overhead... Translucent orbs slide past you on lines of energy... carrying passengers between the bright beacons of silver cities... You follow one at random and watch as it descends into a glass city... filled with incredibly tall spires... The ground is lush with sculptured greenery... interspersed by grids of liquid canals brimming with people suspended above being carried in all directions as they travel to their destination... You alight effortlessly in a glade of minute trees surrounded on all sides by glass spires... In the centre of the glade is a small pool... You walk quietly over to it and look within... As you gaze into the surface... you notice the liquid revolving slowly *round in circles... The movement sinks you into a deep and beautiful trance... and as you are dimly aware of the circles increasing their speed the surrounding dissolve in a kaleidoscope of colours... and you are back on your chair... enveloped in deeply relaxing yellow light.*

JOURNEY INTO ATLANTIS

Imagine yourself at the top of a cliff overlooking a panoramic view of rugged coastline and emerald sea... As you look down... you see a path winding down towards the shoreline... Although the path is steep and is overgrown with spartan trees... the way seems clear... You start down the path... and as you take your first few steps downhill... the next foothold seems to rise up in front of you... as if by magic... illuminating the way... The further downward you descend... the more relaxed you feel... Every step becomes more natural to you as the track winds its way through rocky outcrops and wind-sculptured trees.

As you walk between two large boulders you find yourself in a natural shrine within the rocks... A mandala has been lovingly inscribed into the rock face... and a small cairn at its foot is decorated in flowers... and small offerings from past travellers... You notice a small cave to one side... where a soft bed of straw has been laid out... and you see that anyone who wishes may use this place to rest... Although you could easily stop and spend the night here... you decide to continue down... towards the shoreline below.

You continue down the path... feeling more and more relaxed... as you approach the bottom of the cliff... The rock path soon gives way to luxuriously soft sand... and you feel your feet sink all the way up to their ankles... as you make your way on to level ground... The sand becomes firm as you cross naturally formed rocks to a beautiful rugged coastline... lapped by crystal clear azure waters.

You feel so relaxed and the water look so inviting that you cannot resist removing your clothing... and after filling your lungs with the fresh salt air... you dive deep into the water... As you enter the water you are surprised at how light you feel... The water is so clear you can see the sea floor... heading further and further down towards something that glimmers in the distance... Without thinking about it you immediately head in the direction of the faint glow... It comes as no surprise that you find it easy to breathe... in fact... you feel so secure and rested that your breathing becomes more regular and deeper... As you are drawn to the glow below you... you realise the glow is coming from inside a giant oyster... On reaching the oyster... you see that the glow is caused by a huge pearl sitting at the back of the oyster... Instinctively you are drawn inside the oyster... immediately feeling totally relaxed as you enter and settle on the infinitely soft surface of the oyster's tongue... As you lie down... you gaze into the roof of the oyster above you... It is a perfectly smooth mirror surface of mother-of-pearl and you see yourself reflected in it.

As you lie there feeling completely at home you become aware of someone nearby... You languidly bring yourself into a sitting position and you see a beautiful mermaid floating above the pearl... bathed in its light... it is a wondrous sight and as you watch her... with infinite ease she glides off into the distance. You start to feel a gentle pull calling you towards the surface... In your own time you drift gently back to the surface of the water... and climb back onto the rocks... Enjoying their shade while still feeling the warmth of the sun... as you make your *way leisurely back up the hill... to the shrine you had passed earlier... and settle down on the bed of straw.*

FANTASY STOP-SMOKING AVERSION

To double your resolve you have only to imagine yourself in a beautiful glade of living trees... where you can see each and every leaf on every tree... opening and closing... happily sucking in the sweet aromatic air around them... On the far side of the glade you see a horribly huge fire... it has been purposely lit... and smoke is starting to fill the air... The leaves are shrinking in on themselves... and you imagine their little mouths screaming as they choke on the suffocating air... They start to shrivel under the increasing heat... closing up... attempting to hide from the spreading fire... as it moves relentlessly across the glade... Where the fire has been the leaves and branches are left... dripping with viscous black tar... like oil-soaked birds stuck in an oil slick... The trees are struggling to breathe... unable to move under the heavy weight of their tar-soaked leaves... You eyes are wide in horror as you realise... that left like that... the trees will slowly and painfully die... As the first fire dies from lack of oxygen to feed it... another fire starts up again at the far side of the glade... Suddenly... you realise that the fires are all the cigarettes you have ever smoked... and that the trees are your lungs... Your only hope is to destroy all the cigarettes... that have been in your life... and never... never... start another one. Only by imagining yourself smoking all the cigarettes you have had at once... can you stop this continuing... so you do so... to save your lungs... that they might breathe again... When you have done this... this thought will forever put you off... even the idea of ever smoking again... and polluting your surroundings.

If you wish, you can create your own suggestions. You should be aware that the mind can be very literal when you are in hypnosis, so avoid using words that have double meanings. Keep your suggestions in the present tense. 'You will stop smoking' could be in 20 years' time and your inner mind may keep this suggestion open endlessly.

A few rules that may be worthwhile taking into account when formulating your suggestions:

- Use the present tense
- Be positive
- Be specific
- Be detailed

- Be simple
- Use exciting, imaginative words
- Be realistic
- Personalise the suggestions
- Symbolise your suggestions (imagine yourself as you want to be – a healthy, confident non-smoker, etc.)

Keeping these instructions in mind and taking note of the examples given can help you to create an imaginative suggestion.

5

This chapter includes a variety of reports from around the world. An extensive search was necessary to gather any statistics recorded on hypnotherapy. Hours were spent on the Internet by my colleagues and myself trying to find research figures on stopping smoking and hypnosis, but the information I needed was not forthcoming. As a result, the layperson may think there is no research on the subject. It appears that the evidence is locked away in scholarly journals where access is limited to the medical profession. No wonder leading associations suggest that there is no conclusive research to prove that hypnosis works! Finally in the US, where information is more widely available, I was able to find the stacks of research I wanted – though not without more than a little help from my partner, who himself is a researcher and historian. You will find the results listed in the bibliography – full proof that not only does hypnosis work but that it has a massive documented success rate, leaving all the other products and therapies standing.

Dangers to the smoker

Every year the US tobacco companies handed over their list of top-secret cigarette ingredients to federal officials, who dutifully locked them away. Revealing these ingredients is a criminal offence!

Listed below are just a few of the known 350 poisons in cigarettes. Additives used in American cigarettes are thought to be similar to those on lists prepared by the Canadian and British Companies.

And the radiation, well! You should envy the people that live by Sellafield nuclear energy plant. If you smoke as many as one and a half packs a day, in a year you will be experiencing 1,000 times more radiation than you would if you were living on the doorstep of a nuclear reactor (Ontario, Canada government report).

In the following pages you will find fascinating information extracted from research on smoking that has recently been revealed. And as more information leaks out Americans are now taking stopping smoking very, very seriously, with laws making it illegal to smoke in all public places.

Even if the smoker was able to read the official lists, s/he would still not know what ingredients are added to individual brands. This makes it impossible for a scientist to do accurate research to determine whether certain additives alone or in combination increase the already known considerable risk of smoking.

The tobacco companies' reason for not publicising their ingredients, as quoted by tobacco executives, is 'We are protecting brand recipes that are trade secrets'. However, Dr Kaiseman may have come close to exposing the lethal horrors in fags. In his research in 1992 he found that out of 32 brands of rolling tobacco the quantity of deadly ingredients was unrelated to brand or type – mild, light, or ultra-light had the same amount of lethal ingredients, and the only difference was in the construction of the filters and tubes.

Recently, the European Parliament has been

lobbying to make it illegal to use such terms as mild, light, low tar, etc. However, these findings persuaded an anti-smoking rights association to file a complaint with the Department of Consumer and Corporate Affairs – claiming such labelling was misleading! This led to more research with more refined technology. The only way the tobacco companies could attempt to prove the findings were incorrect would be to reveal what their 'specific' additives are.

If the government wants to cut lung cancer, changing the soil the tobacco is grown in is the best way to do so. 'The radiation soils of Southern Ontario, Georgia, Alabama and Virginia have significantly more radiation than the black soils of China and Turkey', says scientist Dennis O'Dowd.

Fact: The tobacco companies are allowed to put 2% heroin and cocaine in their preparation to treat tobacco.

NARCOTICS IN TOBACCO?

The following anecdote appeared in a recent issue of *The Facts*, by Lendon Smith, MD. From a correspondent in Texas:

A patient of mine told me this story: she lit a cigarette in the presence of her nephew who was visiting her. He took the cigarette, extinguished it in the ashtray and threw both out the back door. Taking her cigarette pack from her purse, he deliberately crumbled each one into the wastebasket, sat down and looked at her without saying a word. She, of course, asked him what he thought he was doing.

He said, 'Auntie, if you have to cut your head off to quit smoking, do it! You'll suffer less in the long run. Remember, I am the chief chemist for a tobacco company. People think they are hooked on nicotine. They don't know we are permitted to put two per cent of habit-forming narcotic in the syrups we use to treat cigarette tobacco. Smokers are hooked on heroin and cocaine, not nicotine.'

Cigarettes are like little furnaces – reaching temperatures of up to 1,200 degrees and many substances become carcinogenic when heated. Harvard University research showed that when you burn some substances they become 25 times more toxic. Walter Ross, a *Reader's Digest* staff writer and editor of *World Smoking and Health*, confirms this in his article, 'What has been added to your cigarette' (July 1982).

The Humectants are what keep cigarettes fresh and the major ones are glycerol and glycols. Glycols are implicated as a risk factor for bladder cancer. On top of that, burning transforms glycerol into acrolein, which in turn suppresses the action of the cilia that expel irritants from the lungs. 'As a result, the smoker's risk of chronic bronchitis and emphysema is increased and the lungs are open to attack by toxins and carcinogens.'

CIGARETTES AND RADIATION

Scientist Dennis O'Dowd says that radioactive by-products released by burning cigarettes are the only elements proven to cause lung cancer. The burning of cigarettes releases radioactive polonium. Polonium isotopes are the daughters of radioactive decay products of radon.

According to an Ontario government study of uranium workers, polonium metal is vaporised by the heat generated by smoking and sucked into the lungs, where the metal is deposited.

It was estimated that smokers of one and a half packs a day are exposed to 8,000 millirems per year (*Science*, December 1984) – far greater than from any other radiation source. As O'Dowd says, your exposure could be several thousand times greater than living next door to the Pickering nuclear reactor in Canada. 'Burn anything, and you concentrate its radioactive component. Radiation uptake by a plant depends on soil exposure,' he observes.

When I first published my book in Malaysia in 1997 the only statistics I could find that prove hypnosis works for stopping smoking, and indeed put hypnosis at the top of the list, are those reported below. I checked the USA, Canada and the Internet and came up with no scientific data reports on proof of hypnosis working. NOT BEING AWARE CAN MAKE THE DIFFERENCE TO YOU BEING A SMOKER OR NOT.

Hypnosis has been scientifically proven to be the most successful method of cessation, even simple suggestion hypnosis. So why is this fact not publicly reported? It is very easy for scientific studies and other data to get lost in the global consciousness when the media have not taken an interest, or are not receiving relevant statistics in the first place. But for whatever reason, the information goes unreported; buried in files and only known to the choice few that happen to read it in established journals such as *New Scientist*.

You may think this sounds a bit steep, but in researching this book I was interested in getting the latest statistics and so used my journalist's hat. I contacted ASH and QUIT, both groups that are funded to help the smoker who wants to give up. QUIT is the UK's main charity organisation whose aim is to offer practical help to people who want to stop smoking. When I asked for statistics they recommended I call ASH (Action on Smoking & Health), as QUIT only functions as an information line. When I asked QUIT if they recommended hypnosis their reply was that they do not encourage hypnosis because there is no scientific research available to substantiate its success. Today they say it works for some but that the individual has to be careful because there is no scientific research available to substantiate its success.

ASH is a charity aimed at producing information for the media, Parliament and the NHS. They gave the same advice. They are also the main contact for the press and media regarding smoking cessation. In fact the buck usually stops there – at

ASH. They are believed to have all the statistics and research figures on smoking cessation.

I requested some figures for the different methods of smoking cessation and received a stack of typed-out reports from a variety of newspapers and journals around the world. And guess what? Not a mention of hypnosis in any of these serious reports on methods of stopping smoking. Hypnosis was not alone; acupuncture was also amongst the therapies left in the dark, as are probably many other new methods. I had often wondered why hypnosis was sometimes missed out of articles altogether, especially when quoting facts on success rates for specific methods of giving up smoking. Even on National Stop Smoking Day, hypnosis was at best given a couple of lines in the press, unless an occasional article focused on it specifically.

I did find dozens of studies on the 'drug-related' stop-smoking products, such as patches, nasal sprays and gum. It seems unrealistic to believe that none of our universities have experimented on hypnosis and produced some statistics, or perhaps it's the £150,000-plus needed to sponsor a scientific double-blind research that prevents the hypnotherapists from getting their own success rate figures out. Even the most successful hypnotherapist would have to treat thousands of clients to pay for such research. Fortunately, I can now give you the results of some studies, easily found by physicians but difficult if you do not receive the scholarly medical journals.

However, I did find a few lines in the booklet QUIT sends out on request to the public. This is a very small booklet that gives you a brief outline of all the products and treatments that are on the market. It is well laid out and easy to read but, alas, very unflattering to hypnotherapy. Hypnotherapy is grouped with alternative therapies that appear at the back of the book. This section begins, 'There's no proof that either hypnosis or acupuncture are effective treatments for smoking cessation. However they do work for some people. There's no harm in trying them.' Hardly an incentive to use hypnosis! It adds insult to injury by suggesting that the reader should be suspicious of claims that as many as 90% of smokers who undergo hypnosis are able to give up smoking, and concludes with, 'Experts say that 40% success rate is the very best that can be expected among people giving up for the first time.' Who are these un-informed experts, I wonder?

The response was almost the same at ASH. This was rather odd, since I had kept a report from *New Scientist* (October 1992), a highly respected trade journal, which began with the line, 'Hypnosis is the most effective way of giving up smoking, according to the largest ever scientific comparison of ways of breaking the habit.' The report was carried out by Frank Schmidt and researcher Chochalingam Viswesvaran of the University of Iowa. They collected statistics from more than 600 studies covering almost 72,000 people in America, Scandinavia and elsewhere in Europe. This combination of studies was the largest ever scientific comparison, and counteracted the defects of small group studies, thereby giving a more correct overall view. The research done on hypnosis was using just an average suggestion therapy, or tapes alone. The analysis of treatment at this level of hypnosis, which included 48 studies covering 6,000 smokers, gave an average success rate of 30%. These figures correspond to the *lowest* success rate in hypnosis given in major hypnosis books, and do not take into account a good script and more modern techniques with semantics.

Christopher Patterson, chairman of the British Society of Medical & Dental Hypnosis at that time, said that *current* hypnosis techniques gave a more positive result of up to 60% using the latest relaxation methods, and from just one single session (that is when relaxation methods meant quite rightfully hypnosis). So even with such basic suggestions, and using the minimum success rate figures, hypnosis is the most successful method for smoking cessation, but still goes unreported as such. Exercise and breathing therapy came next with 29%, while acupuncture achieved 24%. The least successful was advice from GPs, which was only nominally higher than willpower, with a success rate of only 6%. Self-help in the form of advice from books and mail order achieved a modest 9% success rate, while nicotine gum was a little better at 10%. The article states that Richard Doll, the epidemiologist who carried out the pioneering studies on the risks of smoking, said that the apparent success of hypnosis and the high quitting rate of patients with heart disease backed his own observations.

I asked, on several different occasions (between

1990 and 2000) why there were no research figures on hypnosis. Each time I was told virtually the same thing: that there had been no research to substantiate any success rate. Each time I pointed out the article in *New Scientist* ASH were surprised to hear of its existence, and asked me to fax it to them, which I did. I had spoken to David Pollock myself in 1990 for some support on hypnosis. It wasn't forthcoming. The media cannot really be blamed, nor can the staff at these groups, but one might question who is responsible for hypnosis's lowly public profile.

SMOKING INCREASES THE RISK OF A HEART ATTACK BY FIVE TIMES

From a report by Clinical Services Trial Unit:

It is reported that smokers in their thirties and forties suffer five times the number of heart attacks as non-smokers. It shows the latest statistics published in the *Medical Journal* provide the firmest evidence yet that you do not have to be old to suffer a heart attack if you smoke. Twenty thousand Britons a year suffer from heart attacks under the age of 50, and more than 50% of all the attacks are caused by tobacco. 'These figures are far more than previously thought,' said Dr Rory Collins,

British Heart Foundation senior research fellow at Oxford University, and one of the study's organisers. He says that the evidence shows there is no such thing as a safe cigarette, 'They are all good at killing you'. The research, involving almost 14,000 Britons who had survived heart attacks, compared their risk factors with 33,000 relatives, some of whom smoke. If you have a heart attack younger than 50 then there's an 80% chance tobacco caused it.

Professor Richard Peto, of the Imperial Cancer Research Fund, one of the study's backers, said that if you survive your first heart attack, then stopping smoking still makes you much less likely to have another. Research in Finland reported that of 12,000 women who had babies in 1966, a total of 571 died in 1993. Women who smoked after the second month of pregnancy were twice as likely to die early as were non-smokers, and were less likely to give up smoking at all in the future. In fact they were more likely to become even heavier smokers. But if the woman gave up in the first month her risk dropped one and a half times.

Approximately 40% of Europeans now (1994) smoke.

PREGNANCY AND SMOKING – THE FACTS

If you smoke you are at greater risk from:

Having a miscarriage
Your baby being born prematurely
Giving birth to a stillborn child
Your baby dying soon after it has been born
Bleeding

Every year 56,000 pregnant women stop smoking.

The effect on the baby

The chemicals in cigarette smoke reduce the amount of oxygen your baby gets through its umbilical cord, which makes your baby's heart beat faster, resulting in your baby growing more slowly. Your baby will weigh less, which isn't healthy, because smaller babies are much more likely to catch infections and diseases.

If you start smoking again after your baby's birth, every cigarette you or your partner smokes directly affects your child's health. The child is breathing in the smoke from the end of your cigarette, which contains a very high level of tar, nicotine and carbon monoxide. Simply breathing in the smoke is a health risk.

It is recorded that children of smokers suffer many of the same health risks as the adult who has actually lit the cigarette. Children who live with smokers are twice as likely to spend time in hospital for chest illnesses such as bronchitis and pneumonia, asthma and wheezing, and even ear infections.

More time will be spent caring for a sick child and time will be lost from school with sickness. The moment you stop smoking you begin helping your baby have a better chance of survival and health.

Merely cutting back smoking has little effect on the welfare of your baby. Each puff allows thousands of deadly chemicals to enter your baby's bloodstream.

You can depend on the chemicals below existing in your cigarettes, chemicals that you will be giving to your child. Chemicals that you will be subjecting your baby to, as well as yourself:

Carbon monoxide – the lethal gas that comes out of car exhausts
Cyanide, an extremely poisonous substance and slow killer

Butane, which is used to fuel cigarette lighters

Ammonia, found in household cleaners

Pink test stops women smoking in pregnancy

An interesting test was given to pregnant women to help them stop smoking. The test provides women with visual feedback on their nicotine intake. Reagents react with nicotine turning their urine pink – the darker the colour, the heavier the smoking. The results of a pilot study showed that of 14 smokers who were given the test, two had quit by the end of the study and seven had reduced their consumption significantly. Smoking levels among a matching control group not given the test were unchanged.

BLACK PEPPER TEST

Forty-eight cigarette smokers participated in a three-hour session conducted after overnight deprivation from smoking. Subjects were randomly assigned to one of three control groups: one group of smokers puffed on a device that delivered a vapour from essential oil of black pepper; a second group puffed on a device with mint/menthol cartridges; and a third group used a device containing an empty cartridge (placebo). Reported craving for cigarettes was significantly reduced in the pepper control group compared with the other two groups. In addition, negative effects and physical symptoms of anxiety were alleviated in the pepper control group relative to the unflavoured placebo. The intensity of sensations in the chest was also significantly higher for the pepper group. These results support the view that respiratory tract sensations are important in alleviating smoking withdrawal symptoms.

Another experiment between site workers and white-collar employees failed to prove any significant difference in the success rate between the two groups.

All this research, and yet none (until now apparently) to be found on hypnotherapy. A search through the Internet showed little else. Most information indicated no research existed to prove the success of hypnosis. So no wonder hypnosis is not up there in front with the drugs, even though it has a far greater success rate – but of course it is not a replacement drug...

Products on the market for stopping smoking

The success rate of these products varies so much from test to test that I suggest you consider all the facts available. You may find the percentages quite disappointing, but it is the most extensive collection of figures that I have come across to date.

ALTERNATIVE THERAPIES

Hypnosis

Although hypnosis success rates vary tremendously depending on what techniques are used in the hypnosis therapy, therapy at its very worst is still way ahead of anything else on the market. At its best in scientific research, it demonstrated a 94% success rate after a period of eighteen months in research conducted with 1000 people (please see Bibliography).

However, the *New Scientist* published an article in 1992 where it stated that hypnosis had the highest success rate for stopping smoking, at only 30% success rate. It included the grim results of the other products on the market. When I looked into the report, it was on studies using suggestion hypnosis only and even included reports on just sitting and listening to cassette tapes.

Hypnosis deals with both the chemical aspects and the psychological aspects, allowing for greater improvements.

Cost: London £75–£1,000-plus for a one-to-one, one-hour stop-smoking session. Groups can cost as little as £40–£150, but note that the success rate may be between 30%–60%. Private one-to-one sessions can reach the 95% success rate in one session, so prices generally depend on the techniques that work consistently. If the hypnotherapist has a lot of press coverage, the many articles usually give credibility, especially if the journalist is a client. But it really is hard to tell. There are some really good hypnotherapists out there who have a good technique but no marketing skill. I can recommend the people I teach because I teach a specific stop-smoking programme not always well covered, if at all, in some training schools. (See back of the book for Austin Technique information.)

Side effects: None.

Acupuncture

This treatment is a very acceptable way to deal with the inner workings of the body, and certainly has a good success rate, although not nearly as high as hypnotherapy. The success rate reported in *New Scientist* is 24%, which is just below the success rate of aversion therapy at 25%.

Cost: Prices vary depending upon location.

Side effects: Similar to hypnosis, although I have no data on the improper use of the needles.

The following information was compiled from the information given out by QUIT:

DRUGS REPLACED BY DRUGS

(Known as nicotine replacement therapy NRT.)

The following products are designed to replace some of the nicotine that smokers get from smoking, but they do not address the psychological addiction of the drug.

Nicotine Gum

Different from ordinary chewing gum, this can have a bitter taste, especially to begin with, so you may have to persevere in using it. It is important to chew it properly to get the full benefit of using it. The gum comes in two strengths, low (2mg) and full (4mg) and in a choice of flavours. You are directed to chew the gum until it tastes bitter, and then place it between the gum and the side of your mouth for 30 minutes. Nicotine is absorbed through the lining of your mouth. If the urge to smoke has not subsided sufficiently, you may need to use the full strength. I have treated a few clients that have become addicted to either the gum or even gum and cigarette, and were having to use both.

Cost: High strength: Approximately £5.49 for 24 pieces. £18.99 for 105. £15 per week for a period of three months.

Side effects:

Irritation of mouth and throat.

Mild jaw ache, indigestion and nausea.

Denture wearers may have difficulties.

Not to be used if you have a peptic ulcer.

Can be unpleasant to use at first.

Ex-smokers can find it hard to stop using the gum after the three-month period.

Unsightly.

Nicotine Patches

These look like plasters and are stuck on to the arm, chest or back each day. Some are worn for 24 hours and others for 16 hours a day. They come in three strengths and work by enabling nicotine to be slowly absorbed through the skin, and claim the individual may still get urges to smoke, but these are not so strong. The dosage should be reduced as the subject goes through the course. Nicotine levels build up slowly during the day to help keep the cravings away.

Cost: Approx. £16 per week, with a recommendation to use them for three months.

Side effects:

Nausea and indigestion.

Itching and redness of the skin.

Possible nightmares, vivid dreams.

Skin damage, likened to punching holes into a waterbed, affecting our resistance to pollution.

Nicotine lozenges and tablets

These may be bought in many outlets, including chemists. A tablet is dissolved in the mouth and nicotine is slowly absorbed into the body. May be more pleasant than gum but no trials have been done to give an indication of success rate.

Cost: Approximately £15 per week. Recommendation is 30 tablets a day.

Side effects:

Nausea and indigestion.

There is a risk of addiction.

The Inhaler

The inhaler looks like a cigarette holder; a cartridge containing nicotine is placed inside. When the smoker gets a craving, the inhaler is held in the hand, and the individual takes shallow puffs (like a pipe) or deep puffs (like a cigarette). Nicotine is taken into the mouth and the back of the throat but not into the lungs.

Cost: Approximately £5.95 for a starter pack and £19.95 for a week's supply of cartridges.

Side effects:

Nausea and indigestion.

There is a risk of addiction.

Harmless to health but can encourage a psychological addiction.

Nasal Spray

The nicotine nasal spray comes in a bottle with a

nozzle that delivers a dose of nicotine into each nostril. Used 10–15 times a day, the nicotine is quickly absorbed through the lining of the nose. It mimics cigarettes more closely by giving a relatively fast effect. Nasal spray is only available on prescription.

Cost: Approximately £20 per week and should be used for three months.

Side effects:

Irritation to the lining of the nose.

Nausea and indigestion.

Very little difference to smoking a cigarette but more sociably acceptable.

Filters

Filters are designed to eliminate some of the tar and nicotine from cigarette smoke. They are placed on the end of the cigarette, which is then smoked as normal. Smokers tend to compensate by puffing longer and harder or even covering up the filter to stop it working so well.

Cost: Between 60p and £1.20 per pack of 10. Each filter lasts for 5–20 cigarettes.

Side effects: None known.

NON-DRUG REPLACEMENTS

(Hypnosis has a success rate of up to a 94% [see introduction]. Can any other stop-smoking product or therapy come close to this success rate?)

Dummy cigarettes

These products are designed to give a form of taste satisfaction when they are inhaled. They look like cigarettes, but are plastic and are not lit. They last from one week to three months depending on the brand.

Cost: From £2–£10.

Side effects: None reported.

Herbal cigarettes

These are supposed to be used to replace ordinary cigarettes and then are to be cut out gradually. Although there is no nicotine in them, the smoker will still get carbon monoxide and tar from smoking them, although less than would result from smoking tobacco.

Side effects:

Effects from tar and carbon monoxide on your body are likely to be similar to those from tobacco cigarettes.

Dummies

The baby's dummy satisfied Liz Hurley when she tried to give up smoking. However, as mothers will know, it is a nightmare to get the baby out of the habit of sucking a dummy – and that doesn't even have nicotine in!

Side effects:

Unflattering and attracts unwelcome media interest!

The Stop Smoking Tablet

The new stop smoking tablet has only just been launched on the market and it is already reported to have some negative psychological side effects. It may be replacing the nicotine but not the psychological habit. The result has been widely published in the national press: women who have used the drug have started to eat large amounts of candy to satisfy the mental urge to smoke. The tablet is just a physical replacement, and all drugs have side-effects.

6

CASE HISTORIES

When a client has a trauma-based cigarette problem it means that he or she was in a state of shock when they had their first cigarette. However many traumas they have preceding such a trauma makes little difference.

So why is the first cigarette taken in trauma so significant? Why isn't it easy to establish which smoker is which? And why do many smokers go back to smoking at the time of a major trauma? The following cases histories may help you understand. I have added some true stories from clients, which are included to show you how the mind works, and although they may not always seem to be connected to smoking, they are examples to help you understand the whys and wherefores of the impulse to smoke. The trauma-related smoker doesn't necessarily remember the trauma and is therefore difficult to spot. Since only a small percentage of smokers go back to smoking in a trauma situation, eg experiencing a loved one dying. Could guilt create a punishment programme and re-start their smoking habit?

Tom's quality of life

One client, whom I shall call Tom, will always stand out in my mind. He came to my practice to stop smoking. He was about 60 and could hardly breathe without coughing. His throat sounded viciously hoarse. I had a very strange feeling when he was having treatment, and it bothered me enough for me to be able to recall the therapy later. He was a 60-a-day smoker and had been smoking since he was very young. One thing about hypnotherapy is that you always get surprises. The client who seems the easiest is not always the one who is the success. More often it is the really difficult clients, or the ones that seem least likely to succeed, that will stop.

Tom was very polite, but looked very ill. He

booked his wife an appointment for six weeks later. I suppose the time lapse was to see if it worked before she took the plunge. I had many clients in the intervening period and so didn't notice the time passing. Then, out of the blue, I had a message from the reception desk. It was from Tom's wife, who was cancelling her appointment. She said that she would have to cancel because her husband had just died, but to tell Valerie that he was so proud to have given up smoking. He had a happy last few weeks. I was sorry to hear the sad news, but the last remark made me realise how much quality of life is worth. I used this story when I had very depressed clients to deal with. It seemed to put the point across. So many people believe that because they are no longer young their health is no longer important.

A fag after sex!

A client I will call Anne had an unusual smoking problem. She believed she would miss out by not being able to have that cigarette after she had had intercourse. Anne said she enjoyed the cigarette nearly as much as the act itself. She had formed an attachment, like a barnacle, and like a barnacle she would need to pry the cigarette addiction away from her sexual behaviour.

Fortunately, this is simple with hypnosis. I was able to pont out how unpleasant, and what a turn off it was, to a non-smoker. In hypnosis the focus allows you to realise how you actually look, rather than how you believe you look, with a cigarette in your mouth. Don't forget, you are still working on old programmes, which probably started to operate when you first started smoking. If you had been watching Humphrey Bogart, Carole Lombard or the young Madonna, in their exciting romantic roles, cigarette smoking was part of the sophistication, power, satisfaction, bliss, control, happiness, gentleness, total relaxation, and fearlessness. In fact you would see everyone smoking most of the time, while experiencing a variety of emotions. So it's little wonder that you form attachments to certain behaviour patterns – a cigarette after a meal, with a drink, with a lover, as an act of friendship, to be sociable, etc. But the fact is that non-smokers happily go through all these emotions without the need for a cigarette.

A ministerial position

When I was working in Malaysia I was invited to meet the health minister at that time. He had given up smoking himself and was the one who was campaigning for a smoking ban in public places and offices. He had been working very hard on this issue and had met a lot of resistance before it became more widely acceptable. He told me that he had given up because he would be constantly dashing out of meetings for a quick cigarette, and he realised that he was having a problem missing important issues.

My most awkward client

The most awkward client I had was an 80-year-old Indian gentleman in Malaysia. It was the first time I have ever *not* succeeded in putting someone into hypnosis.

I worked from my suite on the executive floor of one of the fine five-star Hotels in Kuala Lumpur. When this gentleman came in to see me, he was hissing so much from his chest I could hardly hear myself speak. He was very overweight, which exacerbated his condition. He looked as though he was going to die at any moment. I explained what was going to happen in hypnosis, and when it was time to put him into hypnosis I asked him to close his eyes and I began the induction. The problem was he was finding it so hard to breathe and the laboured breathing he was left with was so loud, I could not concentrate. I decided on a different tactic, one which I hope I will never have to use again. I told him he may as well open his eyes, and I continued to explain that he was in such bad condition that he would be lucky if he lived at all. I said that not only was he killing himself but he was in such a disgusting state that he could not even do the simplest task in life, which is to breathe. I said, 'I am not going to take your money, but every time you put a cigarette into your mouth, I want you to say to yourself, "I am deliberately putting this poison into my system." ' I bade him goodbye and felt very disappointed in myself.

He was a business associate of a colleague and friend of mine called Hagi Abdul. The next day I got a phone call from Hagi to say that the Indian gentleman had stopped smoking and was telling everyone they shouldn't be smoking either because it was bad for them. In fact, he was acting as if he had had a successful hypnotherapy session and was delighted. He was so happy, he said he would pay me. The payment never came but at least he was a satisfied client.

The smoker that travelled from Japan to quit

A client whom I will call James flew from Japan to the UK to be treated by me. He had heard of me from the huge press coverage I had received in Malaysia. The Malaysian health minister had accepted my Austin Technique for inclusion in their stop-smoking campaign. James was a business tycoon and an extremely heavy smoker. He explained he realised he was using the cigarettes as a crutch, but got panicky before his constant business meetings if he did not have a cigarette around him in the meetings. In fact, he lost his cool.

It hadn't occurred to him that he had already lost his cool when he was constantly searching for a cigarette or a light for his cigarette and getting very agitated if he couldn't find his lighter, or if someone moved his cigarettes. Not exactly the best way to conduct meetings – hardly a poker face! But he had been extraordinarily successful in his line of work and was an extremely intelligent person. This made no difference when he tried to stop smoking

– he had been trying to stop for the previous five years.

The one-hour program was enough; he had no need to return for a back-up, although he had prolonged his stay an extra day, just in case. He said he was more excited about his success with giving up smoking than any of his major takeovers. There could always be another deal, but not another life if he screwed up,

The tipsy client

Sometimes people who come to stop smoking will stop drinking alcohol, if they find it becoming a problem and no longer want to drink. A lady came to see me and admitted she was a little tipsy. She looked and sounded fine so I went ahead with the therapy. She mentioned that she associated smoking with drinking and would be happy to give up both. I explained, as I usually do in this situation, that the one-hour programme does not allow time for the alcohol treatment. I also pointed out that the alcohol problem is usually trauma based and needs about three sessions because of the extra time in regression. However, I said I would add a suggestion in the smoking script and that it may help her if the drinking was not trauma based.

I was about to leave the country at this point. When I returned home I received a fax from her to say not only had she given up smoking in the one hour, but also drinking, and all of her friends were absolutely amazed at her. A few months later she sent me a list of people who wanted to give up smoking. Out of the half-dozen people she booked for me on my return, most of them wanted to stop drinking as well as smoking. They were so surprised at the change in their friend that they wanted a bit of the same thing. They were all in the same social group and found that the constant round of dinners and cocktail parties was taking its toll on their bodies.

Paradise stop-smoking cruises

I had already developed a reputation on the Island of Langkawi for helping people stop smoking and had become consultant to the Holiday Villa Hotel on the island. My clinic in Paradise, I called it. A well-known character on the island was Lyn (his real name), a good-looking captain.

Lyn owned his own lovely sailing yacht, and his business was taking people on sunset cruises around the 100 islands surrounding Langkawi. I actually met him when I joined one of his cruises while on a visit. He was an argumentative drinker and when he drank he would be rude to people; he readily admitted this. Lyn came to me to stop smoking, something that he successfully accomplished, and then had an extra session to stop drinking, which also worked. That was five years ago and he still no longer smokes, or drinks. He became a very good friend and we planned to organise some stop-smoking trips sailing around the private islands and beaches – a day's sailing that incorporated a stop-smoking session. The yacht could comfortably hold 20 people and an English film crew filmed me hypnotising one of the guests, against a background of exquisite beauty – a wonderful experience that is a perfect complement to hypnosis.

The hidden trauma

Because traumas can be eliminated from the *conscious* mind it is very difficult to decide who does have a trauma and who doesn't. Guess work is no good, so you have to be prepared. A client I will call Wendy came to see me with an average 20-a-day smoking habit that started when she was at an airport returning from a trip abroad. She didn't really remember why she started; someone offered her one on the plane. When I took her into hypnosis everything went fine, but she returned for a second back-up – which in effect only lasts half an hour. It's most unusual to have more than one. I found that only about 5% would return for the back-up that was included in the price, and maybe only three people a year for a second. It was so unusual that I didn't even bother charging.

When she returned, I regressed her to the first time she had smoked a cigarette. The story was certainly more involved than she had led me to believe, or even realised herself. The airport scenario was correct, she was returning from a trip, a traumatic trip because she had gone to nurse her grandmother, whom she adored. Her grandmother had died and she was returning home, still in shock, when she was offered the cigarette at the airport bar. She was breaking her heart and a fellow passenger was trying to calm her. When she finally stopped crying he offered her a cigarette. She was 23 years old and had never smoked before. That was the beginning of her habit. I dealt with the trauma and she was then able to stop. When she came out of hypnosis she was very surprised, as she had forgotten it was on that particular trip she had started smoking.

The public schoolboy

This was another case in which the client had no idea his smoking habit was involved with a trauma. He was another person who came for the back-up. Like my son, he had started at school at an early age, simply because all the boys smoked. He had edited out of his mind the initiation ceremony when he was only about six years old at which the new boys' hands were tied behind their backs and they were forced to smoke, and whacked until they did. They were proud later and felt they had become adult by being able to smoke. They then went on to initiate the new, younger boys.

Mike the intellectual

Another client came for stopping smoking and, like so many clients, had lots of other problems that seemed to be attached to the smoking. Sometimes a hypnotherapist may talk the person into having more in-depth therapy because they believe that they will not stop smoking without clearing the other problems first. I have always worked the opposite way, and devised a plan to separate the smoking from any other problems. Therefore, if they come for stop-smoking treatment, that is precisely what they get. I have kept my very high success rate with this strategy, and it has worked very well. This is probably why hypnotherapy is the most successful treatment on the market. It can detach smoking from any problems or traumas, as if they were barnacles being prised away. The smoker that stops with hypnosis will be the same person, with most likely the same problems, but at least they will be a non-smoker.

Sometimes the therapy has some very good side effects, increasing confidence and pride. I had a lovely lady that came for stopping smoking. She was of African descent and had always felt herself to be a failure, though she didn't tell me this at the time. Later she decided to come back for some accelerated learning therapy. It was then she told me she had been able to give up smoking easily, and had no problem doing so. She said because of this she felt for the first time in her life she had achieved something and that it had changed her life. Her confidence had really improved and she felt very happy.

The author's five cigarettes a day (continued from chapter 1)

I had decided to cut down on my alcohol and had used hypnosis to tailor my drinking. It wasn't working the way I had expected, and I was just beginning to realise this. There are many reports that seem to disprove this, usually stating that you have to stop drinking completely, except when using hypnosis.

I had been a very happy social drinker, and I had developed what I can only describe as an allergic reaction to the chemicals in alcohol. As a journalist I had had occasion to interview wine companies and found that they were now chemically maturing the wine, and, I suspect, all alcohol. I was assured that it was cheaper and had no side effects, but the gentleman I was interviewing added, 'If you are stressed then the chemical can make you more angry, and in extreme cases even violent.' I had found a very significant shift in my drinking. I was feeling tired when I drank, became less happy and found that the drink made me more agitated – not usually my nature.

Another unpleasant new side effect was that I was getting a hangover quite often, something I had never before experienced. Unfortunately journalists tend to develop a huge social drinking habit and I had been involved in the profession for several years. I always said that if ever I found I had hangovers after drinking, I would stop. I gave myself a year, just to see if the hangovers persisted. That, of course, was my excuse to continue drinking. I was in the 'couldn't say no to a drink' syndrome. Drinking was no longer working as it had before, so I decided to use hypnosis to organise a better drinking relationship with myself.

My reasoning was that if I limited my drinking to two glasses of champagne in an evening, or in 24 hours, then most people would not want to buy such an expensive drink, and that in itself would cut my alcohol intake down, leaving me to at least enjoy my favourite drink. I was working as a consultant to a large company in London and everyone ended their day by going to the wine bar in the evening.

When I mentioned that I had programmed myself to the maximum of two glasses of champagne a day I had no shortage of offers from my business associates to buy me my quota. But a strange thing happened. I found that I was very tipsy after the two drinks. I would be trying not to slur my words, and was not in a fit state to drive my car. I had been pondering over this new behaviour when the aforementioned author was explaining her five-cigarettes-a-day habit. Her remark that five cigarettes seemed a lot to her changed my thinking about my two glasses of champagne – I was only drinking two glasses of champagne and yet still suffering problems. From that moment I realised that, although the author was having so few cigarettes, she would be thinking most of the time of the next cigarette, and counting the hours until she could have it. However many cigarettes you have, you are a smoker and can have the same problems giving up altogether. I immediately had more hypnosis and changed the script to stopping drinking. You can programme yourself to stop and start depending on your circumstances and lifestyle and the suggestions you use.

Paul the intellectually mischievous smoker

Paul was a highly intelligent person who loved to

play intellectual mind games, but he met his match in hypnosis. He was certainly a challenge for me. Paul didn't give up on the first session because he came at his mother's insistence, but later on, in a back-up session months later, he told me he really had no intention of stopping. However, the treatment had put a doubt in his mind and his attitude gradually changed. At first he felt proud to have got one over on me; he felt he had 'won'. Then, after a while, he began to realise that he sounded weak, rather than strong, when he bragged to his friends that the hypnosis hadn't worked.

The one thing that is certain in advanced hypnotherapy treatment is that the client can only win properly if in fact he loses. He wins if, in this extraordinary sparring of the minds, he beats you. But this is a negative win for him, because he keeps his problem. He wins, with honours, if you beat him in these mind-sparring stakes because it results in him ridding himself of the problem, which is why he is having treatment in the first place.

Paul eventually ventured back and finished the treatment successfully. He was so addicted that when he went to sleep he would wake himself up every few hours to have a cigarette. 'I would wake precisely every two hours, smoke a cigarette and then fall asleep happily for another two hours. Whoever I told laughed, "No one can be that addicted," ' he admitted. Paul stopped after the back-up because now he wanted to.

This book gives you the benefit of my experience to give you the ammunition to help you stop smoking. If you persevere there is no reason why you can't stop. If you do find you still need help you can then seek the help of an advanced hypnotherapist. (I have left an address and telephone number in the back of the book for this purpose.) There are many good hypnotherapists around that have excellent success rates, but even an excellent therapist may not be as confident with a stop-smoking programme. Some hypnotherapy schools do not teach a specific method to deal with smokers. So, if you can, go to a therapist with a reputation for stopping smokers or ask for referrals from the therapist so you can speak to some of their past clients who have stopped smoking. I can offer you a list of therapists around the country who are trained in my methods, so I know they will have a good success rate. But that is only as an afterthought. The main purpose of this book is to give you the opportunity to help yourself at an affordable price. My best wishes for a healthy and happy life.

A BRIEF LOOK AT HYPNOSIS IN THE PAST TWO CENTURIES

1775   Mesmer develops animal magnetism, which is later renamed hypnosis.

1784   Marquis de Puysegur discovers a form of deep trance he calls somnambulism.

1821   First reports of painless surgery in France using magnetism.

1841   James Braid changes the name from magnetism to hypnosis and establishes it as a psychological phenomenon.

1845–53   James Esdaile performs 2,000 operations under hypno-anaesthesia. Some necessitate amputation, but are pain-free.

1883   Freud becomes interested in hypnosis.

1887   Freud begins to practise hypnosis, but only has a few patients as he is not a good practitioner. By 1894 he has completely abandoned it for development of psychoanalysis.

(NB: Jung didn't practise hypnosis, so he belongs in psychology!)

1947   Hypnosis is used by dentists in the USA.

1950   Societies and associations connected with hypnosis start up.

1958   The American Medical Association approves the therapeutic use of hypnosis by physicians.

It took nearly two centuries for hypnosis to be recognised as a therapy by the medical associations and over 30 years later, it still hasn't been fully accepted by the medical profession or the public in general.

STOP SMOKING SUCCESS RATES

95%   Private one-to-one hypnotherapy sessions using the Austin technique.

94%   94% of 1000 people stop smoking with hypnotherapy for 18 months or more. Von Dedenroth, T. (1968) *American Journal of Clinical Hypnosis*

88%   Success with hypnotherapy based on one years' follow up. Kline, M. (1970) *International Journal of Clinical and Experimental Hypnosis*

67-68%   Published research findings by Watkins, Sanders and Crasilneck and Hall for Hypnotherapy.

*60%   Single session hypnosis using latest relatation methods.

*30%   Suggestion hypnosis only or just listening to cassette tapes. (*New Scientist*, 1992)

*29%   Exercise and breathing therapy.

*25%   Aversion therapy

*24%   Acupuncture

20%   Nicotine patches + seeing a counsellor

*10%   Nicotine gum

*6%   Will power alone

* Success rates reported by the *New Scientist*

ABREACTION: A raw emotion that is triggered off when in hypnosis.

DEEPENERS: Specially selected words that form instructions for the purpose of guiding the mind into a much deeper feeling of relaxation in trance. The affirmative scripts can act as deepeners.

HYPNOSIS: Not sleep but a heightened state of awareness, similar to a daydream; can be guided into a hypnotic trance by relaxation techniques or be induced by shock.

HYPNOTHERAPIST: A person who uses therapy while their subject is in hypnosis.

HYPNOTIST: A person who guides another into

hypnosis.

INDUCTION :   A type of script carefully formed to guide the mind into relaxation.

SUGGESTION: Words that encourage the subconscious part of the mind into some sort of participation, either physically or mentally.

TRANCE: Many hypnotherapists do not like this word. I am using it to establish a state of hypnosis I beleive when a person is in a daydream they are also in trance.

BIBILIOGRAPHY

Brown, D. and Fromm, E. (1987). *Hypnosis And Behavioural Medicine*. Hillsdale, NJ, Lawrence Erlbaum.

Crasilneck, H. and Hall, J. (1985). *Clinical Hypnosis: Principles and Applications*. Orlando, Grune and Stratton.

Edgett, J. and Edgett, J.S. (1995). *The Handbook of Hypnotic Phenomena in Psychotherapy*. New York, Brunner/Muzel.

Graff, H. et al. (1966). 'Results of Four Anti-Smoking Therapy Methods', *Pennsylvania Medical Journal*, February, pp39–43.

Grosz, H. (1978). 'Nicotine addiction: Treatment with Medical Hypnosis', *Journal of Indiana State Medical Association, 71*, pp1074–1075 and pp1136–1137.

Hammond, D.C. (1990). *Handbook of Hypnotic Suggestions and Metaphors*. New York, W.W. Norton.

Hartland, J. (1971). *Medical and Dental Hypnosis and Its Clinical Applications*, London, Ballière Tindall.

Hershman, S. (1956). 'Hypnosis and Excessive Smoking', *Journal of Clinical and Experimental Hypnosis, 4*, pp24–29.

Holroyd, J. (1980). 'Hypnosis Treatment for Smoking: An Evaluative Review', *International Journal of Clinical and Experimental Hypnosis, 28*, pp341–357.

Kline, M. (1970). *'The use of extended group hypnotherapy sessions in controlling cigarette habituation'*, International Journal of Clinical and Experimental Hypnosis, *18*, pp270–282.

Kroger, W and Libott, R. (1967). *Thanks Doctor I've Stopped Smoking*. Springfield II, Charles Thomas.

Marlatt, G. (1985). *'Situational determinants of relapse and skill-training interventions'*, Chapters in Marlatt, G and Gordon, J. *Relapse Prevention: Maintenance Strategies in the Treatment of Addictive Behaviours*. New York, Guilford pp71–127.

Nuland, W. and Field, P. (1970). 'Smoking and Hypnosis: A systematic clinical approach', *International Journal of Clinical and Experimental Hypnosis, 18*, pp290–306.

Perry, C. and Mullen, G. (1975). 'The effect of hypnotic susceptibility on reducing smoking behaviour treated by hypnotic technique', *Journal of Clinical Psychology, 31*, pp498–505.

Sanders, S. (1973). 'Mutual group hypnosis and smoking', *American Journal of Clinical Hypnosis, 20*, pp131–135.

Spiegel, H. and Spiegel, D. (1978). *Trance and Treatment*. New York, Basic Books.

Stanton, H. (1978). 'A one-session hypnotic approach to modifying smoking behaviour', *International Journal of Clinical and Experimental Hypnosis, 26*, pp22–29.

Von Dedenroth, T. (1968). 'The use of hypnosis in 1,000 cases of "tobaccomaniacs"', *American Journal of Clinical Hypnosis, 10*, pp381–390.

Watkins, H. (1976). 'Hypnosis and Smoking: A five session approach', *International Journal of Clinical and Experimental Hypnosis, 24* pp381–390.

Watkins, J. (1987). *Hypnotherapeutic Techniques*. New York, Irvington.

OTHER BOOKS PUBLISHED BY VALERIE AUSTIN

Slim While You Sleep, Blake Publishing
Self Hypnosis, Thorsons
Free Yourself From Fear, Thorsons
Hypnosex, re-published by Austin Training Ltd.